# CREDIT
# 911

# CREDIT
# 911

## SECRETS AND STRATEGIES TO SAVING
## YOUR FINANCIAL LIFE

**RODNEY ANDERSON**

WILEY

John Wiley & Sons, Inc.

Published by John Wiley & Sons, Inc., Hoboken, New Jersey.
Published simultaneously in Canada.

For general information on our other products and services or for technical support, please contact our Customer Care Department within the United States at (800) 762-2974, outside the United States at (317) 572-3993 or fax (317) 572-4002.

Wiley also publishes its books in a variety of electronic formats. Some content that appears in print may not be available in electronic books. For more information about Wiley products, visit our web site at www.wiley.com.

*Library of Congress Cataloging-in-Publication Data:*

Anderson, Rodney.
   Credit 911 : secrets and strategies to saving your financial life / Rodney Anderson.
      p.   cm.
   Includes index.
   ISBN 978-0-470-58761-4 (hardback); ISBN 978-0-470-76852-5 (ebk);
   ISBN 978-0-470-76853-2 (ebk); ISBN 978-0-470-76854-9 (ebk)
   1. Personal finance.   I. Title.   II. Title: Credit nine one one.
   HG179.A55975   2010
   332.024'02—dc22

                                                                        2010018282

Printed in the United States of America.
10 9 8 7 6 5 4 3 2 1

*To Kim, my loving wife and number one
cheerleader. Thank you for your constant support
and daily words of encouragement. I love you
more than words can say.*

*To my Mom and Dad, who taught me that
anything is possible through hard work. Your
unconditional love and support through all of the
years of my life are deeply appreciated. I'm blessed
with the best parents in the world.*

*To my beautiful daughters, Sara and Nicole, for
always believing in me and keeping me young.*

*Last, but not least, to my mentor, Mary Callegari,
who inspired me to never give up and to realize
that sometimes, a good kick in the ass is the
best motivation.*

# Contents

| | | |
|---|---|---|
| Foreword | | ix |
| Acknowledgments | | xiii |
| Introduction: Living on the Edge | | 1 |
| Chapter 1 | America's #2 Addiction | 21 |
| Chapter 2 | Plastic Dynamite | 41 |
| Chapter 3 | Affairs of the Wallet: Marriage | 57 |
| Chapter 4 | Affairs of the Wallet: Divorce | 79 |
| Chapter 5 | Collections: Deal with It | 95 |
| Chapter 6 | The Credit System and How It Works | 113 |
| Chapter 7 | Buying Real Estate Is Not a Joke | 129 |
| Chapter 8 | What If I Lose My Castle? | 147 |
| Chapter 9 | Damage Control | 159 |
| Chapter 10 | Bankruptcy: Losing the Battle to Win the War | 175 |
| Chapter 11 | Saving Your Financial Life | 189 |
| About the Author | | 201 |
| Index | | 203 |

# Foreword

In 1997, I wrote in my book *Rich Dad Poor Dad,* "Your home is not an asset." Howls of protest went up around the world. One angry real estate agent sent me a note saying, "You are a quack. You should not write financial books. And you call yourself a real estate investor. Your advice is bad advice."

In 2002, my book *Rich Dad's Prophecy* was released. *Prophecy* warned about the biggest stock market crash in history, a crash that is still coming. Obviously, the book was trashed by the financial press, Wall Street, financial planners, stockbrokers, and of course, our banks. On page 7 of *Prophecy* I stated:

> You may have up to the year 2010 to become prepared. In fact, in this book you will find out why the chances are pretty good that between now and the year 2010, there will be another giant stock market boom . . . the big boom before the big bust.

As predicted in *Rich Dad's Prophecy,* on October 9, 2002, the Dow hit a low of 7,286 and the next boom was on.

In 2007, the party ended and we are now in a global hangover, a hangover of debt.

Eerily, on October 9, 2007, the Dow hit an all-time high of 14,164 and then crashed. The global financial crisis was on, a crisis caused by mountains of debt.

In 2010, Rodney Anderson is releasing his book, *Credit 911.* As stated in *Rich Dad's Prophecy,* you have till 2010 to be prepared. Rodney's book is an essential read for anyone who wants to be prepared for the next crash.

# FOREWORD

The primary reason why *Credit 911* is essential is because our money is no longer money backed by gold. After 1971, all money became debt. Anyone who does not understand the significance of this change in our monetary system will be doomed and punished financially. Today, we must all understand money, debt, and credit if we are to survive and thrive financially.

If you are one of those buried by your own mountain of debt, you must read my friend Rodney Anderson's book, *Credit 911.*

Even if you are *not* buried by debt, if you want to get ahead financially and not be a victim of the 1971 change in the rules of money, you must read *Credit 911.*

How did this all start?

In 1971, President Nixon tipped the first domino when he changed the rules of money; he took the dollar off the gold standard. It was one of the biggest changes in world history and a leading cause of today's financial crisis. Nixon turned the dollar from gold into debt. For the economy to expand, you and I had to get into debt. Every time the economy sagged, or politicians wanted to get reelected, they made it easier for you and me to get into more debt. In the 1980s, the debt problems and bank bailouts were measured in millions of dollars. By the 1990s, the debt and bailout problems were measured in billions, and today the problems are measured in trillions. What comes after trillions?

If you are in debt, are struggling to make ends meet, have seen your home decline in value, have lost money in the stock market, are worried about losing your job or home, or are concerned about your long-term financial survival, you have been affected by Nixon's decision to take the dollar off the gold standard.

The banks of the world began flooding the global economy with mountains of money, and the party was on. Easy money caused inflation. Wages could not keep up with rising prices. To make up for this loss of purchasing power, normally sane people became gamblers in the stock and real estate markets. As stock and real estate prices rose, sane people became insane.

## Foreword

After the stock market crash in 2000 and the terrorist attack on 9/11, government and banking leaders began running the printing presses at high speed. Soon hot money was flowing all over the world. The stock markets boomed and homeowners became millionaires as the prices of their homes climbed. Not wanting to be left behind, people with no financial education became real estate agents, real estate flippers, or day traders in the stock market. Between 2000 and 2007, free credit cards came in the mail, saving rates went to subzero, and homeowners used their homes as ATMs.

You see, I love debt, but good debt—debt that makes you richer, not poorer. Learning to use debt was an essential lesson from my rich dad. For you to get ahead financially, you must understand debt, both good and bad, which is why this book, *Credit 911*, is essential to your future. You see, used properly, debt can give you life. Used improperly, debt is financial suicide.

In closing, the year 2010 has arrived. The question is: Are you prepared for a world buried under mountains of debt?

—Robert Kiyosaki

# Acknowledgments

The writing of *Credit 911* has been a long road—one filled with excitement, long hours, hard work, brain-numbing wordplay, minor setbacks, major victories, and countless interviews with people in crisis. I've experienced growth as a man, husband, father, leader, and educator.

I owe a huge thank-you to my co-worker and friend, Suzie Reed, without whom *Credit 911* would not have been possible. When you first walked into my office eight years ago, I could never have known the impact you'd have on my life and my career. Thank you for always pushing me to do more, and believing that we can accomplish great things together. Thank you for always doing whatever it takes to get a job done, and for the countless nights and weekends you've sacrificed for our cause. I look forward to many more years, many more books, and moving mountains together.

I never understood the true meaning of "fighting the good fight" until my friend Charlie Turano came into my life. Charlie, your positive outlook on life and continuous encouragement have supported me through the toughest of days, and each time I leave your company, I leave with a sense of confidence that my life holds limitless possibilities. No challenge is too great, and the good guy does prevail. Thank you, Charlie, for the guidance you've shown based on your vast experience, for your faith in my project, and for looking out for me when I was busy looking out for everyone else. Mostly, I thank you for your loyalty and your friendship.

Thank you to former congressman Larry LaRocco for showing me that one man can make a difference. Navigating the political arena in Washington, D.C., in support of HR3421, Larry was instrumental in getting my idea turned into a bill and introduced to the House of Representatives and the Senate in an effort to help millions of Americans struggling with medical collection debt. Without his guidance and support, this bill may never have come to fruition. Larry, I'm forever grateful for your believing in me, and for turning my idea into reality, and feel that I've made a lifelong friend in the process.

Thank you to my trusted advisor, Tom Kalahar, whose constant coaching and analysis of all things media and beyond, boosted me to the next level. I am so grateful to you for recognizing the magnitude of our potential, and for the support you've shown throughout this process. You are greatly appreciated.

To my friends Greg Ray, Michelle Lemons, and Michael Broussard at International Speakers Bureau and ISB New Media, I thank you for believing in me and for all of the time and input you've contributed to *Credit 911*. Your feedback and honest analysis of the work helped to make this book possible, and I know there are many other meaningful projects ahead.

To Debby Englander, Kelly O'Connor, Adrianna Johnson, Claire Wesley and all contributors at John Wiley & Sons, I thank you for your tireless work on *Credit 911*, and for believing in my message. You are true professionals, and I am very grateful for all of your guidance and support.

# INTRODUCTION

# Living on the Edge

It amazes me how easy it is to ruin perfectly good credit with one ill-advised decision. It happens every day, even to people who have paid everything on time for years, played by the rules, and avoided risky or dangerous money habits. One of the problems in our system is that your credit rating is tenuous and can change very quickly (on the downside); but it takes forever to repair a problem and to move your score back up.

## Bad Credit Happens to Good People

I want to share a few examples with you to make the point about how we are all living on the edge when it comes to credit. First is the case of the typical hard-working American following the rules and maintaining an excellent credit rating:

### Bad Advice Is Easy to Find

Dave was a 34-year-old teacher with a wife and three children. He and his family had been sacrificing and following a strict budget for years, saving to buy their first home. Along the way, Dave had built up an outstanding credit score of 797—good enough to be pre-approved for a home loan. When he was ready to buy, Dave and his wife found the perfect house in a great community. Everything was falling into place, and 30 days before closing, it looked like their dream was finally within reach.

Then Dave walked into a Bank of America branch to make a simple deposit that would change his life. In years past, a bank teller would have just processed the transaction, handed Dave his deposit slip, and said, "Have a nice day." But now tellers are trained to cross-sell their bank's menu of financial products, and in this case the offer of the day was a credit card. The teller asked Dave if he would like to apply for a new credit card with the bank, and he said, "No thanks, I've got too many credit cards already." The teller went into hard-sell mode and told Dave he would be wise to get rid of his existing credit cards and go with the bank's product. Payments would be easier, money would be saved—he was very convincing. In Dave's mind, since the offer was being made by a respectable, well-dressed employee at a prestigious bank, it felt more like a hot tip from a financial professional than a sales pitch. Dave followed the advice, closed his credit cards— and promptly dropped his credit rating from a stellar 797 to a not-so-wonderful 627. As a result, Dave failed to qualify for a home loan.

**911 SECRETS**  Never take financial advice from anyone unless you have proven they are qualified to give it.

One minute he was a shoo-in for a loan that would enable him to buy the home of his dreams, and the next he was plunged into the nightmare of bad credit. He and his wife were devastated. A routine trip to the bank had shattered all their hopes for a better life. The house they had fallen in love with the moment they saw it— gone. The wonderful school district they had carefully picked out for their kids—gone. Instead of entering an exciting new chapter in their lives, Dave and his family were back to square one. How could this have happened?

The bank teller wasn't deliberately looking to sabotage Dave's credit. He was only trying to supplement his $24,000-a-year salary with additional commission. The odds are, he had no clue that closing credit cards was a terrible idea. There's no way the bank told him to advise clients to close their credit cards, so where did he get the fatal misinformation? I would be willing to bet the original source was one of the so-called financial experts on television, who are constantly yelling, "Close your accounts! Cut up your credit cards!" They make their living offering tips on the stock market and a host of other financial subjects, and for years, millions of Americans have been heeding their advice as if it were gospel. And yet, even though most of these experts lacked the foresight to predict the mortgage disaster that has plunged us into a crippling recession, they are still on the air, and huge audiences are still hanging on their every word. It's like a doctor failing to diagnose an obvious medical problem until it is too late to treat the patient—the difference is that a doctor is subject to a malpractice claim that might ruin him or her, whereas the financial expert can simply shrug and deflect any criticism with lame excuses like, "Hey, we were all fooled," or, "No risk, no reward."

911 SECRETS

Be aware that your adviser has a financial stake in the advice he or she provides. Remember, he or she makes money on that advice. Make sure you fare as well or better than your adviser does.

The problem is that most of us assume a financial expert wouldn't be offering their advice unless it was sound. But nothing could be further from the truth. A celebrity financial guru on a cable program might have a personal stake in recommending certain types of investments or might just be wrong too often to help the investors who rely on his or her opinions. Either way, the average American is not getting rich from following their advice, and many have been hurt by it. As an alternative to relying on unreliable stock tips, I want people to make informed decisions, understand the rules of the game, and become more self-reliant when it comes to improving their financial strength. And that's precisely the goal of this book.

## You Had Better Shop Around

I've talked often about the subtleties of financial advice, but there's nothing subtle about being hustled, and the cutthroat marketplace of today is a breeding ground for shady business practices. Anyone can be victimized, no matter how educated or experienced they might be. A great example was that of the lady who was tricked into a subprime loan even though her credit rating was excellent.

911 SECRETS

Never—never—assume that a professional will not hustle you just because of the prestige of their position. Prestige often is the refuge of the worst scoundrels. Let's not forget the once highly prestigious Bernie Madoff.

### The Old Bait and Switch

Caroline came into my office with her husband. They had recently moved into a new house, and they wanted to refinance their loan, which was at a high rate of interest. Caroline was a successful attorney, she and her husband made over $250,000 a year between them, and their credit was flawless. I asked, "Caroline, why on earth are you in a subprime loan?" She looked sick to her stomach as she explained, "We were supposed to get a 30-year fixed-rate loan. Everything we owned was packed up in moving trucks and ready to roll, but at the closing, when I sat down at the table to look over the paperwork, I noticed the loan documents were not for the 30-year fixed loan we had negotiated, but for a two-year adjustable—I was in shock. I immediately called our loan officer, but his voicemail picked up. So I called the company directly—and got more voicemail. Nobody was around who could help me. Nobody was reachable by cell. It was the middle of the afternoon, and yet there was not a single person around to explain to me what was going on."

In other words, the loan officer had pulled a bait and switch on Caroline, and now he was lying low. Caroline was beside herself with anger and frustration. We couldn't postpone the move," she went on, "and the trucks were costing us $3,500 a day. We were stuck—and that's how we ended up with a two-year adjustable loan." Think about that for a second. She's a lawyer, trained to never sign a document unless everything is perfect, but she picked the wrong mortgage broker and ended up being saddled with the wrong loan with the worst possible terms even though she qualified for the best terms available. Worse than that, property values fluctuate all the time, and if Caroline's went down, she might have lost the opportunity to refinance. No refinancing option means higher mortgage rates and higher payments, and suddenly Caroline's carefully calculated budget would be shot to pieces.

The only way to protect yourself against this happening is by getting everything in writing; set the terms, and *walk away* as soon as those terms are changed. In the long run, you're better off delaying the closing to get the financing you deserve or just walking away. A mortgage loan is a long-term commitment, and your best bet is to ensure you're using the right, trustworthy, and experienced lender up front to prevent ending up in Caroline's predicament.

911 SECRETS

Always be on the lookout for the bait-and-switch. If the terms change midstream, STOP. Delay the closing or walk away, but never sign under pressure.

The resulting snowball effect could have led to Caroline and her husband struggling to keep up with payments, and even going into default—a complete disaster. It was not Caroline's fault—she thought the loan officer had been "very nice," and she assumed she would get the loan she had bargained for and to which she was entitled. But her predicament demonstrates why every decision you make in your financial life is very important and can lead to long-term consequences. Just being intelligent and experienced isn't enough anymore. You need to become financially street smart, and that's where I come in.

## Why You Should Listen to Me

Bad financial advice is given every day to millions of hard-working Americans, and not just by bank employees chasing a sales commission or by TV talking heads trying to fill up an hour of programming and push their sponsors' agendas. It's being spouted by a range of "professionals" working throughout the financial services industry.

Closing your accounts and cutting up your credit cards may seem like sensible advice to someone trying to get a handle on their debt, especially when it's coming from people who look and sound like experts. But the consequences of following bad financial advice can be catastrophic. The only way to avoid this all-too-common hazard is to arm yourself with the relevant facts about your credit and finances, and by the end of this book, you will be armed to the teeth—that's my mission.

The first step in the process is scaring you into a little healthy skepticism about the credentials and motives of anyone offering any kind of financial advice. For example, right now you should be asking yourself what qualifies Rodney Anderson to save anyone's financial life. After all, I am a mortgage lender, a job description that's become almost a dirty word lately. Well, I didn't start out in the mortgage business. My first job out of high school was working as a teller in a bank, and I was just as clueless and inexperienced as the teller who convinced Dave to destroy his credit. I was also married at 21 and a father of two by the time I was 23, and looking to buy a home. Our credit was shaky, but just good enough to secure a loan—the wrong loan. It was adjustable, and it kept adjusting itself upward. We couldn't refinance because our house just didn't have the value, but eventually I met the right lender who put us in the right loan. That was a revelation. Eventually, I became a loan officer, trying to make enough in salary and commissions to survive while paying off $60,000 in credit card debt.

Then my wife and I got divorced. It was a very difficult time, but it was also a learning experience—not just emotionally, but financially. In fact, I have devoted an entire chapter to the financial repercussions of divorce because so many people are going through it and yet so few of them understand how to protect their credit interests.

By the time I got into the mortgage-lending business, I had personally been through most of the issues covered in this book. Being able to relate to these credit difficulties and financial challenges definitely helped sensitize me to the circumstances faced by mortgage applicants every day. But in my first lending job, I was also blessed with an amazing mentor who never let me forget that mortgage lending is an opportunity to help others, and that your clients' needs should always be your top priority.

As a lender, I've been examining the financial backgrounds of loan applicants for nearly two decades, and in doing so, have learned literally everything there is to know about the world of credit. Before that, while working for years down in the trenches of the banking industry, I had a ringside seat for most of the important economic developments of the past 25 years. I witnessed the S&L scandals unfolding back in the late '80s and early '90s. I saw the banking industry gradually shift from promoting savings products to pushing credit products. I watched helplessly as the mortgage bubble grew rapidly on a foundation of bad debt and then exploded in the face of the American public—I saw it coming but could only stand by and await the inevitable. I watched as lenders began cooking up loan products that were destined to fail. I saw the tactics of greed in my industry evolve to the point where hardly any lenders had the integrity and common sense to say "No" to a loan applicant, regardless of credit or earning capacity.

That's the thing that really struck me: Suddenly, the answer was never "No." I want to help people realize their dream of home ownership, but if I said "Yes" to everyone who came through my door, pretty soon I'd be responsible for a lot of foreclosures, bankruptcies, stress, divorce, and all around misery. My company turns away loan applicants by the bushel. We will not sell a loan that isn't a good fit for the client—period. If an applicant's credit isn't good enough, that's that. I don't say, "No," but I do say, "Not yet," and I give them the tools to improve their credit so they can try again.

The success of my company reflects the truth of the old saying that honesty is the best policy. Repeat customers and referral business are the foundation of my company. After all these years, I'm still putting my clients first, and it works.

## Don't Blame the Swimmers as They Drown

Throughout the book I use the stories of real people coping with real-life credit scenarios to illustrate my lessons because they provide a human context to which we can all relate. Some of you will read these stories and think, "Well, it serves 'em right. They got in over their heads. They shouldn't have taken mortgages they can't afford, they shouldn't max out their credit cards, and they shouldn't live beyond their means. People should be more responsible."

There is definitely some truth to this perspective, but it's a superficial truth that misses the larger reality beneath the surface. It's true that many Americans spend more than they earn. Millions have taken high-interest mortgages that busted their budgets. Millions more routinely charge purchases that load their credit card accounts with debt.

But the credit crisis isn't just an issue of personal responsibility. That's part of the problem—and I address that issue in my seminars— but it's not the whole story. Let's face it: Millions of American wage earners live paycheck to paycheck. A huge percentage of these folks use credit cards just to fill the gaps. Maybe their kids need some clothes. Maybe their car's transmission has given out. Maybe their roof has started to leak. Maybe someone in the family has gotten sick and racked up medical bills that insurance doesn't cover. These aren't uncommon scenarios. While it's true that many people try to "keep up with the Joneses," it's also true that most are simply trying to keep their heads above water. To complicate matters, many credit card companies charge interest rates that defy almost anyone's ability to keep up. Is it any wonder that Americans feel as if they're drowning in debt? Tell me honestly: if you call people irresponsible as they drown, is that going to save them?

Most people agree that we're currently facing the most dangerous financial crisis since the Great Depression. They're right—it's the credit equivalent of an 8.5 magnitude earthquake. The credit situation in this country is already a disaster for many Americans; a major threat to others; and a long-term problem for almost everyone. The subprime mortgage debacle was the initial tremor, but the numerous aftershocks are doing most of the damage. Lenders have drastically tightened their guidelines, meaning millions of responsible, hardworking people can no longer qualify for loans. Millions more are suffering foreclosure, bankruptcy, or both, while those fortunate enough to acquire loans are paying much higher rates than before.

**911 SECRETS**

There are no "get out of jail free" cards when it comes to borrowing money. The lenders are the judge, jury, and executioner.

Meanwhile, countless credit cards are maxed out, and defaults are through the roof, causing severe and widespread credit damage across the country. Even people with excellent credit have cause to worry as we move forward into an uncertain economic future. The only thing that's certain is that maintaining good credit is more essential than ever to our financial survival.

## Statistics Don't Lie—But They Can Scare You Half to Death

What have the current financial "experts" done for you so far? Let's take a look at the numbers:

- By 2012, an estimated 7 million homes will have been foreclosed in a five-year period—that's over a million homes a year.
- At least 5 million personal bankruptcies will have been filed in that same five-year period.
- In addition, 144 million adult Americans have not had their credit pulled in the last year—that means nearly half the people in this country have no idea where their credit stands.
- One in every four homeowners in this country is "upside-down" on their mortgage, owing more on the property than it is worth.
- From 2008 to 2009, 15 percent of American adults, or nearly 34 million people, were late making a credit card payment and 8 percent (18 million people) missed a payment entirely.
- In 2009, college seniors graduated with an average credit card debt of more than $4,100, up from $2,900 almost four years before. Close to one-fifth of seniors carried balances greater than $7,000.
- Credit and debit card fraud is the number one fear of Americans in the midst of the global financial crisis—worse than terrorism and personal safety.
- 92.5 million American adults grade themselves a C, D, or F on their knowledge of personal finance.
- A full 40 percent of American families spend more than they earn, greatly increasing their risk of foreclosure, repossession, and bankruptcy—setbacks that can lead in turn to a greater incidence of divorce, health issues, and other forms of stress on families.
- The total amount of consumer debt in the United States is currently more than $2.5 trillion.
- More than 20 percent of Americans have "maxed out" their credit cards.

- 27 percent of Americans over age 45 are putting their retirement on hold.
- Among Americans over 50, 45 percent say food prices are causing a budget hardship, and 39 percent expect they will have to ration food in their future. As a result, many of this group will need to come out of retirement to supplement their income.*

I could go on. If these statistics prove anything, it's that Americans need better financial advice than they've been getting. So much for the "experts."

## The Only Thing Worse Than No Advice Is Bad Advice

You have probably seen the signs reading that "Bad advice and dumb looks are free." But think about it: Would you ever order a subprime steak? Would you send your kids to a subprime school? Would you bring your car to a subprime mechanic? Of course you wouldn't. So why do we Americans continue to accept subprime advice regarding our mortgages, credit management, financial planning, investments, insurance, and every other economically significant aspect of our lives?

The truth is, until now we have trusted too many so-called experts motivated more by their own pocketbooks than by ours, and this misplaced trust can really hurt us. I call it subprime advice because I think the best example of what can go wrong when we follow bad advice is the collapse of the subprime mortgage market. There are basically two kinds of subprime advice: professional subprime advice and brother-in-law subprime advice. Professional subprime advice is the kind of advice we get from people who are motivated by some factor other than our own best financial interests—like the advice offered to Dave by the bank teller. Then there is the brother-in-law variety, which is the kind of advice we get from friends and family who might mean well but don't really know what they are talking

---

* Alex Johnson, "Economy hitting the elderly especially hard," *MSNBC,* July 28, 2008.

about. Don't let the fact that the person offering this kind of advice has been through what you are going through—remember, just because your brother-in-law survived an appendectomy doesn't mean he's qualified to perform one on you.

911 SECRETS

In most cases, in-laws, cousins, uncles, and "a guy I know" are not the best sources for financial advice.

Another category of bad financial advice goes beyond the realm of "subprime." It's what I call "predatory" advice. As the name suggests, this is the kind of financial advice forced upon us by ruthless types trying to exploit our financial ignorance or desperation in an attempt to make a quick buck at our expense—think Bernie Madoff. But he's just the tip of the iceberg. I had one elderly client recently who was retired and relied on his investments for income, who told me his broker had his entire portfolio invested in stocks. I told him he should switch brokers, and he was reluctant. He'd been using this same broker for a long time. He trusted him, and he thought he was a "nice guy." I said, "Well, Ed, either switch brokers or cash in your portfolio and go play roulette in Vegas with the money—you'll get the same odds." That broker recommending all stocks to an income investor was Predatory Advice 101. He was gambling all of Ed's money on high-risk investments because he stood to make higher commissions. Some of these brokers also encourage investors to borrow on "margin," which is essentially borrowing against the value of your investment portfolio.

To avoid this problem, work only with a financial adviser who charges a flat fee but does not earn commission for the advice they give you. If any of your money goes into stocks or mutual funds, you can execute those orders on your own, using an online discount broker. A financial adviser who does not earn commissions is much more likely to give you advice aimed at protecting and improving your situation.

An example of financial risk you face daily is a predatory lender who takes a client who can afford a $120,000 home and convinces him to buy the $400,000 mansion instead. The reason is simple: the higher the loan, the higher the lender's commission. Never mind that the borrower can't afford the loan—the lender gets his big commission and moves on to the next victim.

## What You Don't Know *Can* Hurt You

With all that subprime and predatory advice floating around, it's no wonder so many of us are getting ripped off constantly and in a dozen different ways. I know—I hear the stories all day long. For example, a guy named Dan called in to my radio show. Dan had a great credit rating. Then the company where he works announced that they would not be paying any more bonuses for the time being. Dan decided he needed to save some money, so he called his mortgage servicer one day to get a mortgage modification. You'll never believe what they told him. They said he needed to go 30 days behind on his mortgage in order to get the modification. So what did he do? He followed the bank's instructions and went 30 days late on his mortgage payment.

Dan got his modification, all right, but as a consequence of getting a month behind on his mortgage, his credit score dropped 200 points. This bumped his credit card interest rate up from 7.0 percent to 34.9 percent—and wiped out the money he saved on his mortgage modification. Not only is that a prime example of subprime advice, but it also underscores the importance of your credit score and how one innocent mistake can drive it into the ground, no matter how spotless your record was before the mistake.

When someone gives you advice that just doesn't sound right, listen to your instincts. Remember, long after your adviser has gone on to other clients you will still suffer the consequences when the advice fails you.

Like it or not, your credit is your financial identity in the eyes of the world. Is it fair to be held accountable for years because of one innocent mistake? No, but that's the way it works. Most people know they have a credit score, but don't understand how it works. They think it's just sitting there, and every now and then it gets adjusted when some major financial swing occurs in their lives. Wrong. Credit scores go up and down constantly, and there's a very long list of ways to impact your credit. The good news is that by the time you finish this book, you're going to know everything you need to know about achieving your maximum credit rating and keeping it that way.

It all starts with avoiding bad advice and misinformation that leads to mistakes that hurt you. I get calls on my radio show every week from people who have heard wrong information repeated so many times that it takes a lot of effort to set them straight. I remember one caller who was convinced that debit cards and secured credit cards are the same thing. They're not the same at all, but the caller had heard otherwise enough times to tell me I was wrong. Another recent myth is the idea that debit cards are foolproof, indispensable, and the only way to spend money without risk. This myth originated—surprise—with the banks that issue the debit cards.

You should use your debit card for every purchase, said the banks. Why? They claim they wanted to protect you from credit card overuse and the dangers of carrying around cash, but the real reason was to compel you to overuse your debit card and incur overdraft fees. With everyone running around using debit cards, the banks could count on a huge profit from overdraft charges. Before someone finally raised the alarm and put pressure on the bank to curb stealth overdraft practices, the banking industry reaped billions of dollars a year.

The infallibility of the debit card is a myth, but it's also just another form of subprime advice, and by accepting the sales propaganda of the credit and banking industries, you're giving someone license to steal your money. You should always assume the worst when it comes to financial products that sound too good to be true. By the time the alarm was raised over stealth overdraft practices, the banks had already pocketed billions. But don't worry, they'll think of something else to replace it. You can protect yourself by being prepared for whatever comes along.

 Many credit issues are the result of people believing something that sounds too good to be true. Remember, if it sounds too good to be true, it probably is.

Sometimes, it isn't bad advice that is ripping us off—it's silence. For instance, Eric came into my office to apply for a loan, and as I was looking over his financials, I noticed that he was overpaying for homeowner's insurance. Most people haven't got a clue if their rate is too high, but I'm in the mortgage business, so I can spot an inflated rate a mile away. I asked Eric when he had last spoken to his insurance agent. He couldn't' remember. Then I asked Eric if his agent ever called *him*. He said no, he had never called. I referred Eric to another agent to get a better rate. Eric called the other agent, and presto, his premium dropped from $2,200 to $1,133 per year. But the kicker is that the lower rate actually originated from the *same* insurance company he'd already been using. He realized he had wasted thousands of dollars over the past several years that could have paid for his child's college tuition.

Insurance agents are not in any hurry to call you and give you a lower rate, so they play possum and hope *you* never call *them*. That's silent subprime advice—unless you ask, they won't tell. That goes for all types of insurance, and many people have at least three different insurance policies, so if they don't pick up the phone and call about the rates for all of them, that's giving someone a license to steal your money, times three.

This book gives you the secrets and strategies you need to save your financial life. Our lives are governed by credit because we live in a credit economy. Your credit and your credit scores are huge factors in your life from the age of twenty-one until the day you die.

If you ignore this reality, you're sunk. As you can see, there are lots of ways you can damage your credit without even knowing, and believe me, I've only scratched the surface. I encourage you to become credit conscious and to become smarter in your financial life. After you read this book, you'll have the ability to recognize missteps before they happen.

 You cannot get rid of credit problems by dropping out of the credit economy, because that's where we all live. You have to learn the rules, not try to skirt around them.

Erase all of that subprime advice from your mind and replace it with information and strategies that will help you thrive in the credit world. It's more than just spotting subprime advice. It's more than just becoming credit savvy. It involves changing your approach to the way you spend your money and make financial decisions. This book explains the various sources of credit problems, identifies those problems that affect you the most, and offers solutions that help stabilize and rebuild your credit. So far I've given you a few examples of how important your credit score is and some of the many ways it can make or break us. The rest of the book goes into more detail about the credit challenges, shows you how to fix what's broken, and gives you the tools to control your own credit destiny. Below are chapter summaries dealing with all the major and minor credit issues you need to know about:

*Chapter* 1: *America's #2 Addiction.* This chapter describes the epidemic of spending that has contributed to the current credit crisis. I'll talk about the explosion of what I call "impulse shopping" since the coming of the Internet age, and why having eBay and Craig's List, and thousands of other online shopping sites, at our fingertips, 24 hours a day, has made shopping monsters out of so many of us. This chapter helps you distinguish needs from wants, schedule your online shopping to avoid periods of vulnerability, and, when you absolutely must make a purchase, train yourself to use payment methods that won't add to your credit woes.

*Chapter 2*: *Plastic Dynamite.* Here I focus on those little slabs of plastic dynamite you carry around in your wallets and pocketbooks—credit cards. I reveal the tactics and come-ons used by the credit card companies to lure in customers who have no business owning too many credit cards. I show how your interest rates can go through the roof in a heartbeat over the slightest delay in payment, and how a default will trigger obnoxious phone calls from dawn to dusk. I also show you how to defend yourself by understanding how the credit card companies work and how to avoid falling for their tricks, how to set up a system to monitor accounts, how to track payments and pay on time, and recognize that the credit bureaus hold your financial life in their hands. This chapter teaches you about "credit chasing," where credit card companies lower your limit as you pay down the balance, and shows you how to read between the lines of credit card company advertising, to see their "rewards" programs for what they are: an attempt to get you to overspend on a card disguised as a "membership benefit." You will see that the credit card companies are the predators, and you are the prey. This section shows you how to survive and thrive in the credit jungle.

*Chapter 3*: *Affairs of the Wallet: Marriage.* This chapter explains the 10 things you must do before you say "I do." I examine the unique set of credit problems that come with marriage. For anyone thinking about getting married, full disclosure *before* entering the legal contract can save your financial life and in some cases, save you from complete ruin. When you marry someone with past credit problems, those problems can become yours. This chapter shows you why it is so critical to ensure you find the *financial* Mr. or Mrs. Right.

*Chapter* 4: *Affairs of the Wallet: Divorce.* This is a *must-read* chapter for anyone going through marital discord. Divorce happens to more than half of all marriages. In this chapter I address a common problem that many divorced people are simply not aware of until it's too late. In the urgency to get closure and a final end to a marriage gone bad, people assume that the signed court order is the last step. This is not the case. So many people thought they were divorced only to discover that the marital contract does not go away so easily; if you have any jointly owned property or obligations, you need to make sure you truly cut the ties. This chapter provides you with the action plan you need to make sure that you get divorced in both legal *and* financial terms.

*Chapter* 5: *Collections: Deal with It.* This chapter tackles one of the biggest sources of stress in the life of the credit-challenged: the collection agency. It causes problems at work. It causes problems at home. For some, it makes just waking up in the morning a chore. This chapter gives you the secrets and strategies you need to keep collection agencies at bay. It helps you handle aggressive collection agents, shows you how to speak their language, and offers you solutions to your predicament.

*Chapter* 6: *The Credit System and How it Works.* In this chapter you find the intricacies of a system that is not designed to be user-friendly but which holds the power of life and death over your financial identity. This chapter alone is going to forever change the way you handle your finances—and the way the marketplace handles you. Among other things, Chapter 6 shows you:

- How the score system works and common pitfalls to avoid
- How to learn your score and understand what it means
- How your score is calculated, and what you can do to maximize it

- Credit capacity—the fastest way to raise your score
- Credit point system—understanding the math
- How to set short and long-term goals for managing your credit

*Chapter 7: Buying Real Estate Is Not a Joke.* A real estate agent can make or break a deal, and this chapter stresses the importance of working with the right agent as well as the right lender. I show you the ways realtors and lenders operate, and give you a list of must-ask questions to use when selecting both. Buying real estate is a huge investment, and can be a confusing process, so professional representation is imperative. This chapter shows you why real estate agents wield so much power in the transaction, and why it's so important to know you've selected the right one.

*Chapter 8: What if I Lose My Castle?* Here you discover how to avoid foreclosure and how to provide comfort and rebounding strategies if you have already suffered the loss of your home. I explain the pros and cons of the choices available to you so that you'll know which option makes the most sense for your situation.

*Chapter 9: Damage Control.* Here you see why we are all statistically likely to suffer a major financial setback at some point in our lives, and what you need to do to protect yourself. I cover insurance, investments, and identity theft. This chapter is a summary of everything you need to guard against and prepare for a financial catastrophe.

*Chapter 10: Bankruptcy—Losing the Battle to Win the War.* This chapter helps you determine when bankruptcy is right for you, which debts can be included, and the questions you need to ask before hiring a bankruptcy attorney. It also shows you how to reestablish your credit afterward, the do's and don'ts, and the resources available to you. Timing is everything, and you need to know how to get through bankruptcy while keeping recovery in sight.

*Chapter* 11: *Saving Your Financial Life.* The last chapter empowers you to translate your dreams, energy, and good intentions into dollars in your pocket. Here you learn about assigning a family chief financial officer (CFO) as a credit, debt, and investment monitor. You will see how to set measurable goals in the areas that will impact your life. No matter what you are going through right now, there is a light at the end of the tunnel—I've never seen an obstacle to financial stability and security that couldn't be overcome.

911 SECRETS

You gain financial freedom by taking control of your finances and by living within your means. That's it.

Too many people have become credit statistics. They didn't have to be, and you can avoid it entirely. Even if you have great credit or believe that you understand the credit system well enough, there is information throughout this book that allows you to keep what you have and reach higher financial goals than you ever thought possible. All you need are the resources, the insights, and the solutions to the problems that get in the way, and this book empowers you to take control of your financial life.

# CHAPTER 1

# America's #2 Addiction

Shopping. For many, it is the real American dream, the addiction that compels people to buy things they don't need and worse, can't afford. Like all addictions, shopping can become addictive and may even cause psychological problems beyond ruined credit. Ask any recovering drug addict: You are likely to hear how drugs ruined all of their relationships and devastated them. Could a shopping addiction create the same kinds of problems? Absolutely.

Our credit system has made it so easy that for some it becomes irresistible. The desire for instant gratification tricks these poor souls into years of financial enslavement, and the credit card companies and other lenders become the taskmasters of the American dream turned to nightmare.

## The Seduction

Have you ever had a one-night stand? The kind where you buy an outfit for one night, and then it stands in the closet for the rest of your life? How many impulse purchases have you made that fit this description? For most people, the answer is "plenty." The real question here is, How often do you suspend your financial judgment when you get caught up in the thrill of the shopping moment? Marketers count on you doing just that every time you look at one of their products. And lately, it's not just the shopaholics who are vulnerable—it's everyone.

Part of the reason for this financial trap is the slick, high-tech, psychological warfare that the advertising industry has used in recent years. But the root cause of our spendthrift consumerism is the rise of the credit card. It used to be that even the most effective advertisement could only capture a market made up of people who could afford the product—but not any more. The days of slick, cleverly crafted ads, of the Madison Avenue ad executives (*Mad Men*), are gone. It also used to be the case that only creditworthy applicants could get a credit card, but now even infants and toddlers receive preapproved credit card applications in the mail. It's all just too easy.

You can get anything you want *right now*—a house, a car, lots of furniture, electronic gadgets, a closet full of clothes, you name it—and you don't even have to pay up front or even for up to a year later. Companies eagerly seduce you into buying now, paying later. And you'll pay, and pay, and pay. The sellers' seduction techniques get you in the door and coax you into making commitments you have no business making, to buy products you don't need, and didn't want until they convinced you otherwise.

To make matters worse—for the consumer—you now have to deal with a trend in marketing that I call "Size Does Matter." Everyone is trying to sell us bigger, better, fancier stuff, and that means more expensive stuff, and whatever they're doing, it's working: The fast-food expression "Supersize me" is the new consumer motto, and it applies to everything. Thanks to easy credit and powerful marketing campaigns, we all buy bigger stuff—and more stuff—than we need, and we spend more than we can afford.

**911 SECRETS** Always be aware of the words *bigger, better, more*: these words define how many Americans overbuy and fall into the trap of living beyond their means.

How did we fall for this? It's because "marketing" is really just a nice word for the emotional and intellectual manipulation advertisers use to influence our spending habits. The credit card companies want us to spend; it seems the government does, too. Remember those stimulus checks the federal government sent out? The idea behind that plan was to get people *spending*, not saving. It's not just credit card companies and the government. Manufacturers also want us to spend. When the economy is sluggish, the government seems to believe that spending solves everything. The marketing of the constant advances in technology puts a lot of pressure on consumers to keep upgrading, regardless of cost, and this plays right into the hallowed American tradition of "keeping up with the Joneses." For example, having an enormous flat screen TV in your living room is practically a domestic requirement these days. Teens and even younger kids feel pressure to own the latest iPhone and home gaming system. Every month, some new high-tech toy becomes the "must have" item of the moment, and marketers make sure that we feel the need to own the item right away so that we pay top dollar for it. We could wait a few months until prices come down, but by then, the cutting-edge thrill is gone. We must have it *now*, even if it means maxing out a credit card. In hindsight, we shouldn't be too hard on ourselves—these marketers are very, very good at what they do, and having access to easy credit has made us even more vulnerable to their tactics.

## Shop around the Clock

Being in the mortgage lending business gives me a front-row seat to observe the state of economy. I am constantly evaluating the creditworthiness of a huge cross-section of American consumers, reviewing their financial information and listening to their stories. My job also requires that I know what's happening in banking and credit circles, and where things are headed. From my vantage point, I see a growing crisis in our country, and it gets worse every time we turn on our computers and connect to the Internet. As good as the marketers and credit card companies are at influencing our spending habits, they probably couldn't have done such a thorough job of transforming the American consumer into a spending machine without the emergence of online shopping.

Over the past decade or so, millions of previously frugal and responsible consumers have been sucked in to the online shopping vortex. In a shopping 2.0 environment, the mall is always open, and online impulse buying can be as addictive as gambling or any other vice you can name. Until recently, you had to get in the car and drive somewhere in order to shop. The time and effort involved not only limited how often and where you went shopping, but also made you evaluate your purchases a little more carefully than you do when you are browsing the Internet. Now you can sit in your underwear and shop while you eat breakfast, or shop while you're at the office, or shop late at night when all the stores are closed.

Don't feel like battling the retail store crowds on "Black Friday"? No problem. The first Monday after Thanksgiving has now been designated as "Cyber Monday"—as if we needed another excuse to go online and overspend. This is just the latest development in a trend that's been in the works for a long time. When I was a teenager, I worked in a department store that was open Monday through Friday from 10:00 A.M. to 9:00 P.M., Saturdays from 10:00 to 6:00, and Sundays from 12:00 to 6:00; the store closed on holidays. I remember when Walgreen's announced they would stay open on Christmas Day—it was a pretty big deal. Other stores followed suit, staying open later and later, until eventually, many were running 24 hours a day, seven days a week, including holidays. And then along came online shopping.

Internet spending now accounts for tens of billions of dollars a year in sales and is growing exponentially—and that means billions of dollars in credit card charges. The result is millions of Americans saddled with inflated credit card interest they can never hope to pay down. Online shopping options are unlimited, creating a marketplace so full of temptations that not even the strongest of us can resist all of them.

A perfect illustration is what happened to Bob. He'd always been careful about spending and stayed within his budget. He used his credit cards sparingly and never missed a payment on them. Then Bob discovered the online auction site called eBay. At first, he was happy just surfing around the site, marveling at all the amazing things that people were buying and selling. Then late one night, he saw something he'd always wanted but never dreamed he would ever own: an original Civil War battle flag. It was very expensive, but Bob didn't care. He had plenty of room on both his credit cards, so he leaned forward and hit the "Buy It Now" button. A chill went down his spine as the words "Congratulations! You just bought this item!" flashed across the screen. Bob was in heaven—at the touch of a button, his lifelong fantasy of owning a piece of history came true. When the flag arrived later that week, it was everything Bob had hoped it would be and more. And then he went back on eBay, just to see what else was out there. Within six months, Bob had acquired a large and impressive Civil War artifact collection—and over $20,000 in credit card debt. His monthly payments skyrocketed. He started making payments late, and then started missing them altogether. Within another six months, Bob had defaulted on both credit cards and was being hounded by two obnoxious and aggressive collection agencies. The same thing happened to a woman I know who starting buying 20 pairs of shoes every day. She just went online and started buying, keeping the habit up for months. Sound familiar?

**911 SECRETS**

You need to resist to survive. Remember those words of wisdom, "I can resist everything except temptation." Source: Oscar Wilde, *Lady Windermere's Fan*, 1892.

Repeatedly splurging on a private indulgence and ending up deep in debt is bad enough. But people have become so comfortable with online shopping that they think nothing of buying cars, boats, and even real estate online—three areas where careful research and in-person inspection are absolutely essential to avoid getting bamboozled. Yet millions of dollars of real estate are sold every year on the Internet, unseen by the buyer. I know a couple who did just that—they went online and bought a house in what the listing called "a great neighborhood in a cozy suburb" of a city about a hundred miles from where they lived. When they finally showed up to have a look at their investment, they saw to their horror that the house was right in the middle of a seedy, crime-infested area, and when they got out of the car, they heard gunfire a few blocks away. They got back in the car and sped off, never to return—and were stuck with a house they could never resell.

## What Happens in Vegas Stays on Your Credit Report

As I've said many times, online shopping can be as addictive as gambling, and apparently, so can online gambling. There are over 500 online poker tournament sites out there, each of them hosting hundreds of games a day to the tune of millions of dollars a year. Many of these card players are young people with credit cards they probably shouldn't have, and the results are predictable.

**911 SECRETS** In the world of gambling, losers *always* outnumber winners. Always.

I'll never forget the morning I received a frantic phone call from Cindy. She said she needed to see me right away to set up a cash-out refinance on the house she'd owned for 15 years. I scheduled an appointment for later that day—when there's a rush to refinance, it means someone's in trouble, and I could hear it in her voice. She arrived half an hour early for her appointment, looking distraught and pacing back and forth. I asked her to tell me the purpose of the cash out. She sat down and said, "I could lie to you or I could tell you the truth." I told her to give it to me straight. She took a deep breath and began her story.

Her son had called her up the day before, saying he needed $40,000 and quickly. Cindy was stunned, and asked her son for an explanation. He told her, "Mom, I'm addicted to online poker, and I'm $40,000 in debt. I've maxed out my credit cards, and I'm thirty days late on one of them." Cindy couldn't believe it. Her son had never had a gambling problem or any other addiction in his life. And now, here he was, up to his ears in debt from playing online poker—she didn't even know there was such a thing. Her son had a great job with a defense contractor, but the position required security clearance that involved routine credit checks. The head of Human Resources (HR) for the company was saying that if her son didn't clear up the debt immediately, he would have to be let go.

Cindy feared this would ruin her son's future, and she knew if he got fired, she would end up supporting him. So she came to me for a cash-out refinance—a way of raising money quickly using the equity in her home. She hated to do it, and I hated for her to have to do it, but she was a desperate parent trying to protect her child, so I understood.

Cindy's predicament made me stop and think for the first time about what a dangerous place the Internet can be. Gambling used to require travel and effort to keep it an occasional pastime for most Americans, just like frivolous shopping. Once the Internet was added to the mix, the floodgates of addiction were opened for an entire culture.

## Did You Ever Get the Feeling You're Being Watched?

For those of you who grew up watching *Sesame Street*, the cute little characters often had equally cute names. But today, a different kind of "Cookie Monster" is out there, and, yes, it is watching you.

About two months after my meeting with Cindy, I was making a follow-up phone call to a mortgage applicant named Brian. He was surprised to hear from me. He said he "already spoke to the mortgage guy yesterday." I said, "Brian, nobody from my office called you yesterday." There was a pause. "Then who called me?" asked Brian, obviously embarrassed and totally confused.

What happened was that when Brian applied with me for a loan and I pulled his credit report, it created what is called a "trigger lead." This means that a credit bureau, knowing Brian was in the market for a loan, sold his name and number to another mortgage lender, who then called Brian in hopes of catching him off guard by simply identifying themselves as "the mortgage company." Sounds underhanded, but it's not illegal, and it's done all the time. Anyone who has applied for a loan or who already has one gets mail and phone calls constantly from "your lender" or a representative, or so they say. With everything automated, the identification of a lender's name often leads to unintentionally humorous mistakes. For example, one client with a mortgage written by Charles Schwab Bank began getting phone calls from someone who was offering refinance terms; they said they were calling from Schwab Charles.

The flood of predatory calls to get you to refinance or to steal you away from the lender you're working with gets even worse. In a way, the Internet marketplace is the biggest Ponzi scheme of all time. What I mean by this is that everyone who's selling or advertising something online relies on Google and other search engines to give their product visibility. Most people looking online for things simply type it into Google and use the top five or so search results as the basis of their purchase. A lot of us assume that these top five results are there because they are the sites that have received the most visits from consumers, and therefore are probably the best or at least the most popular. In the early days of Google and Yahoo!, this was an accurate assumption, but no longer. Now companies pay big bucks for search engine optimization, and the company shelling out the most money gets to be at the top of the page, or "above the fold," as they say.

**911 SECRETS**

In the game of online shopping, know that the marketers are always one move ahead of you.

What this all means is that not only is the Internet a constant temptation to overspend, but its reliability as a source of the best deals, the best products, and the best services has been hopelessly compromised by competitive bidding for corporate visibility. Ironically, the same companies using the Internet to leapfrog ahead of their competition are also vulnerable to Internet abuse. Their employees may work for them, but they are also individuals with their own online addictions, and countless man-hours are lost each year to online loitering in the workplace. In response, many companies have started monitoring Internet use by employees, but the more determined online junkies avoid detection by bringing their own laptops, blackberries, and iPhones to work with them. No doubt about it: we're hooked, and we're all visible now.

Another disturbing reality about the Internet is that every time you search for something online, you are helping to define your spending preferences for thousands of companies who keep tabs on your shopping habits. The notorious *cookie* tracks where you go, what you buy, and what you view. Among other things, this system leads to individually tailored pop-up ads and e-mails from companies that sell the products you want. That's like walking into a mall and being followed around by a group of salespeople who take notes on everything you buy or even step in front of you and block your way while they force their sales pitch down your throat.

Since the Internet and all its temptations are not going away—ever—and because you can rely on corporate America to continue to use the Internet to their advantage and at our expense, you need to attack the problem realistically. There's no magic cure here—you have your own spending weaknesses, and you probably can't afford to just turn off the computer indefinitely. The only way to get a handle on the problem is to admit to yourself that the problem exists and be smarter about how you approach the Internet.

Hopefully, just knowing you're being manipulated every time you log on will make you think twice about all those offers and deals that pop up on your screen. Also, being familiar with the tactics that are being used helps you avoid many of the traps that have been set for your wallet. But it's a numbers game, and sooner or later, hanging around online is going to cost you—unless you're prepared. By following the guidelines and suggestions below, you can continue to spend time on the Internet without risking your financial stability.

### You Really Want It, but Do You Really Need It?

The first step is learning to distinguish your needs from your wants. Ask yourself: Is it a necessity? Am I addicted to buying this kind of item? Have I overspent on similar items in the past? Is this the only one in existence, or are there plenty more where that one came from? Most important of all, you must honestly answer the question, "Can I live without it?" In most cases, the answer to this last question is "yes," and if that's the case, then let it go. Keep moving. Don't look back. There will be other opportunities. Remind yourself that each time you pass up a must-have, you are strengthening your resolve that much more, and that each time it will get a little easier to resist the temptation. Once you've turned your back on enough must-have items, you'll stop thinking in terms of must-haves altogether and start treating purchases for what they are: potential investments of your hard-earned money and credit.

### Shop for the Item, Not the Convenience

Even if you decide an item is a need, you still have to approach the purchase intelligently, which means never buying an item solely because of its convenience. Convenience is a factor, but there are many others to consider before buying. Also, whether you are shopping for the perfect pair of shoes, a digital camera, or a vacation home, remember that no matter how great something may look on the Internet, there's a good chance it will fit, feel, and appear differently in person. Using shoes as an example, keep in mind that a size 7 shoe from Gucci will fit differently than a size 7 shoe from Ferragamo. Even the same size shoe from the same maker may fit differently. Shoes are best when tried on for size. With digital cameras and other electronic devices, on the other hand, you need to research the item a little before committing.

One thing about the Internet is that it is crammed with people's opinions about every subject under the sun, including the pros and cons of consumer products. Use this as a resource to get a sense of whether the item you are considering has been well received by consumers. Compare prices—one seller of a particular item may be charging double or triple what others are charging. And remember, as convenient as online shopping might be, returning items bought on the Internet can be a nightmare, so check the return policy of the seller with whom you are dealing. When it comes to real estate and other major purchases, forget about convenience—get up off the couch and go inspect the potential purchase yourself. There's just no way you can ever hope to buy a house or a car sight-unseen without ending up disappointed, or even ripped off. Apart from training yourself to be a careful shopper, following all of these steps will also duplicate the "cooling-off" period that is otherwise missing from online shopping.

### Think about Your Purchase for 24 Hours

Remember, any investment of your hard-earned money is worth sleeping on for a night. So many of the items we buy impulsively online only seemed like a good idea at the time, but if we condition ourselves to wait a while before committing to a purchase, we can at least know the decision wasn't made blindly, and there's a good chance we'll reconsider a lot of the more frivolous items.

31

### *Don't Shop out Of Boredom or Depression, and Never Shop Late at Night*

There is something about sitting in front of the glowing screen of the online marketplace late at night that brings out the impulse buyer in us. Perhaps we had a long, trying day and feel as though we deserve to treat ourselves, or maybe we're a little down and the idea of indulging in a purchase or two seems like the perfect antidote. Perhaps we're just bored or not thinking clearly out of exhaustion. Whatever the reason, late-night shopping online is never a good idea, so avoid it. Also, if you have a serious online overspending problem, you shouldn't log on even in broad daylight unless there's someone in the room with you—just their presence can diminish the urge to buy something.

Boredom can lead to destroying your credit. If you feel bored, go to the gym, walk your dog, or call your mom, but don't turn on your computer to go shopping.

### *Make the Payment When You Make the Purchase*

If you have found the object of your desire on the Internet and are ready to make the purchase, be sure you are ready to make the payment. I'm not suggesting you pull out your credit card—that isn't paying, that's just promising to make the payment later. Take out your cash, your checkbook, or your debit card and pay for it with a way that does not increase your debt and makes you feel the financial impact of your purchase immediately. This is a far more healthy way of spending than charging the item and not worrying about the cost until your credit card statement shows up. It keeps purchases in the "now," which is where they need to be if you want to control your own financial destiny.

**911 SECRETS** Pay as you go—what a concept! It would solve so many credit problems we face, and it's such a simple idea.

### *Stay Away from Online Auction Bidding Wars*

If you've ever spent any time on an online auction site, you have no doubt been involved in a few bidding wars. And when you were the last bidder standing, you probably jumped up from the keyboard, pumped your fist in the air, and felt like a champion as time expired. You won! The problem is that people can get so hooked on winning auctions that the thrill of victory becomes the focus and not the purchase itself. Most items start out with an irresistibly low opening bid, which attracts the bargain hunter in you. Then you start bidding, which brings in other bidders who have been holding back but see your bid and think it must be a worthwhile item, or are simply competitive and want to win—sometimes at any cost. For a while, the price is still amazingly low, and you keep bidding just enough to be in the lead—and so do other bidders. Soon the price is approaching the retail value of the item, but by now, you are determined to beat out the competition. In the end, you win, but only when the victory fever wears off do you realize you just overpaid for some furniture you could have done without.

The solution is to avoid bidding wars completely—they create a false sense of urgency to own the item at any cost. Be honest and ask yourself whether you're bidding for items or for the win. The best approach is to observe the "One Bid Rule"—place a bid, if you must, but just one bid at a level you know is a good price for the item, or at least an amount you know you can afford. If you make a second bid, you're opening the door to a third bid, and a fourth bid, and so on. If the item is popular, the chances are you will be outbid at the last second by an auction "sniper," anyway, but don't feel bad—if it is not a unique item, then you may well see a carbon copy of the item for sale by the same seller the next day.

The bidding game is usually driven by other buyers like you who simply want the item, but ultimately it is just a way for sellers to make certain they get a good price for their item. Occasionally, the person you are bidding against is the actual seller or someone working for them, so beware of "shill" bidding done under a second user name. The seller opens a second account and enters bids "against" himself to get the rest of the bidders juiced up, with the idea that this will drive the price upward. It works.

The bottom line is that bidding for an item online is rarely a guarantee that you're getting the best price for that item—the auction price can be influenced by any number of factors—how many trigger-happy bidders happen to be on the web site at that moment, whether a similar item sold recently and for how much, and what time of day or night the auction ended. With those variables, your chances at a real bargain are slim. Remember, when it comes to bidding in online auctions, your mantra should be "One Bid or None."

Don't let yourself be drawn into "auction fever." It might be fun at first but it's an expensive habit. Auctions are like financial opium.

### Read the Fine Print Carefully

This is vintage good advice that few people follow, but for buying online, it's a must. Yes, the excitement that comes with purchasing something you want on the Internet is undeniable, but don't forget that what you have really done is entered into a binding contract with the seller. Once you pay for the item, you anxiously await its arrival, crossing your fingers and hoping it shows up in one piece and as described. And if it doesn't, what are your options in regards to returning the item for a replacement or getting your money back?

If you're buying something from a big company and not an individual, you need to know before you pay whether the seller has a decent customer service department. Did you ever call an online seller's customer service number to complain? There are a few that are helpful, but in most cases your call gets sent overseas to an out-source phone service employee reading from a script—and you get nowhere. If you ask to speak to a supervisor, they put you on hold for 15 minutes and then turn you over to a senior script reader with the same result. This is why it's vital that you understand the item descriptions and sale terms, because they often contain loopholes that the seller can use to avoid responsibility for undisclosed defects or even failure of an item to show up.

You're probably used to skimming most of the terms and conditions that accompany a sale, but with online shopping, you *must* read everything very carefully and ask the seller questions where terms are vague or confusing. In a department store, a dissatisfied customer can frequently get around unfavorable terms and return policies through face-to-face negotiations; conversely, online sellers are faceless and remote, and returns are much more of a hassle for them than for a department store, so they are far less likely to give you leeway on a purchase. At the same time, returning an online purchase is also a hassle for the consumer—finding the right box, packing material, a trip to the post office, and paying postage, all discourage you from going through the process. You're much better off doing your homework in advance and winding up with the right item that doesn't need to be returned.

### Wipe Out Those Cookies

Whenever you go to a web site, a cookie is set up to track where you go and what you buy. These accumulate in your "cookies folder" and the temporary Internet files as part of your browsing history. You need to delete all of these files periodically. The more sites you visit, the more often you need to go to that "Tools" link at the top of the browser page and get rid of all of those files. At least this makes it necessary for the "cookie monsters" to start tracking you all over again. Don't make it easy for them; delete your browsing history frequently.

### Out of Sight, Out of Mind

For those of you who have a very serious online shopping problem, following these guidelines may not be enough to keep you from falling off the wagon every time you're alone with Internet access. If you belong in this category, you need to go a step further. Parents of preteens have the option of modifying their Internet service to restrict online availability to kid-friendly sites, and it is possible to restrict your own Internet access in a way that blocks the sites for which you have a particular weakness. You can block out specific sites like eBay or Craigslist, but don't let anyone talk you into buying the overpriced software that does the job for you. You can do it yourself in a matter of minutes by simply following the steps below:

**For Windows Users**

**Step 1:** Click the Start button and select Run.

**Step 2:** Type the following text into the Run box:

**notepad c:\WINDOWS\system32\drivers\etc\hosts**

**Step 3:** You will see a new notepad window on the screen with information that might be confusing—ignore it. Just go to the last line of the file, hit the enter key, and type the web site you'd like to block in the following format:

**127.0.0.1** ebay.com

**127.0.0.1** craigslist.com

**Step 4:** Save the file, exit, and you're done. The web sites you entered will not be able to open on your home computer. You can add as many as you need to and restore the web sites at any time by opening the same file as in Step 1 and deleting the sites you blocked.

**For Mac Users**

**Step 1:** Open the system preferences pane. There is a short-cut on the dock that is shaped like a gear and says "System Preferences."

**Step 2:** Locate "Parental Controls," and select it by clicking the icon with the mouse. If you have multiple user accounts enabled, you will be able to choose the account that you wish to apply restrictions to. Enter a password if necessary.

**Step 3:** Click "Enable Parental Controls." This will bring you to the main menu for setting the parental control parameters for the Safari Web browser and other programs on the Mac.

**Step 4:** Located the "Content" tab and click on it. Next, under Safari select the type of restrictions that you would like to enable. If you want to create a list of acceptable sites, select the option to "Allow Access to only These Websites." Enter the names of the web sites that you want to allow Safari to access in the table provided. When you are finished, exit Parental Controls/System Preferences and your changes will automatically be saved. The Safari Web browser will now only allow access to the web sites that you have specified.

Although these are self-imposed restrictions that you can reverse at any time, the idea is that the effort and remorse associated with picking your own lock will help deter you. It's important to remove the immediate temptations until you've adjusted to life without frivolous purchases. Treat online shopping like any other addiction and stay away from weaknesses until you're strong enough to resist on your own.

### Designate a "Mall Cop" to Monitor Your Shopping Habits

It may sound over the top, but appointing a family member or friend to help steer you away from trouble just makes good sense. Try scheduling your shopping, and only do it with a companion who knows your habits. Make a list of what you need before getting in the car or going online, and give it to your "mall cop" to check off as you go. In other words, decide what to buy ahead of time instead of going shopping just to see what is being offered. This rule works for everything from grocery shopping to online purchases.

911 SECRETS

Just as you shouldn't grocery shop when you're hungry, don't make online purchases when you're bored.

When you've finished the list, shopping is over. It might be hard at first, but keep at it until you've settled into a routine. You managed to get used to overspending, so you can get used to restraining yourself. Also, having a relative or friend along is an opportunity to turn the process of changing your habits into an enjoyable activity.

### Never Pay More Than You Have to for Anything; Do Your Homework to Find the Best Price

Remember, overspending comes in many forms, and although I emphasize the credit hazards of overspending on *wants*, it's just as important to be a smart shopper when you are in the market for *needs*. If you're looking for an essential item, don't assume that the first search result on Google is the best choice—shop around, compare prices, and take your time. Check independent consumer guides for the best deals and the best quality. Be proactive—don't wait for the marketers to come to you and sell on their own terms.

Your goal should be to overcome any bad financial habits, not to take all the fun out of your life. You don't want to go cold turkey on the frivolous impulse buys, but that doesn't mean you have to avoid recreational shopping forever. I've talked to a lot of reformed impulse spenders who now enjoy window-shopping on a regular basis without making actual purchases. When you think about it, impulse buying is mostly about the "thrill of the hunt" anyway, and you can still enjoy that as often as you like.

Remember that overspending on wants, binge shopping, and online impulse buying is very common these days, so you're in good company. Having a shopping addiction doesn't mean you're a bad person. Nowadays consumers are getting hit over the head all the time with clever marketing ploys coming from many different directions all at once—the banks, credit card companies, manufacturers, and retailers of the thousands of products now available to you in the round-the-clock marketplace. You're only human and shouldn't be too hard on yourself for lacking the will to resist being manipulated by expert manipulators. But as the saying goes, "Fool me once, shame on you; fool me twice, shame on me." Now that you know you're being manipulated, there's no excuse to let it go on. Once you know the tactics used on you by companies, you can develop a healthy skepticism about spending that you will carry with you for the rest of your life. Out-of-control spending almost always leads to a credit-rating casualty, and without good credit, true prosperity is all but impossible.

**911 SECRETS** Never allow yourself to take credit problems lightly. The loss of good credit is a form of financial suicide, and you cannot afford it.

Think of overspending not only as a waste of money, but also as a direct threat to your credit score. Think of your credit as the foundation of your ability to get what you want in life. There are many ways to damage your credit; some are easier to avoid than others, and overspending is by far the easiest. If you follow these suggestions for curbing your spending habits and making smarter choices, it can be even easier.

CHAPTER

**2**

# Plastic Dynamite

I've seen marriages torn apart, families in crisis, and individuals pushed to the brink of despair and ruin by credit card debt. I've had clients plead with me not to disclose their credit card obligations to their spouses. I've watched helplessly as credit card debt skyrocketed on college campuses across the country, quickly becoming the number one cause of student drop out. I've witnessed the dreams of thousands of people go up in smoke, casualties of the no-holds-barred war being waged by credit card companies against their cardholders.

During my weekly radio show, our switchboard is lit up from start to finish with calls from desperate people looking for answers to tough financial challenges, but the one I'll never forget came from a homeowner who paid off a $40,000 second mortgage with a credit card. He only did this, he said, because he received a letter in the mail from Bank of America offering him a new credit card at 0 percent. He figured he could save the 7.9 percent he was paying on the mortgage by shifting the debt to a 0 percent card.

**911 SECRETS** Don't be fooled by 0 percent offers. Introductory rates never last forever. They inevitably expire and end up as expensive offers you can't afford.

He made this transaction, thinking he had finally beaten the system, and celebrated by taking his wife out to a fancy dinner. But 90 days later, he received another letter from Bank of America. This time, the bank informed him that his 0 percent interest rate was being increased to 34.9 percent, effective immediately. He went from paying 7.9 percent on the mortgage balance to owing $40,000 at 34.9 percent, and he was praying he could refinance the debt. Unfortunately, his timing turned out to be as poor as his judgment, because tighter lending guidelines had been imposed and he missed the possibility of a refinance lifeline by a matter of weeks.

By responding to a junk mail bank offer and failing to read the fine print, he was indefinitely stuck with a growing mountain of debt. What happened to his 0 percent? Simple: when he gobbled up all of the available credit on his new 0 percent card, it pushed his credit capacity up to 100 percent, which in turn pushed him into a much higher risk category that meant immediately incurring sky-high interest rates.

Believe it or not, the spectacle of millions of Americans losing their credit posture comes as no surprise to the credit card companies and their partner banks. They encourage us all to charge every purchase we make, and they barrage us with dozens of product come-ons each year. They exploit the vulnerability and naïveté of college students with gimmicky offers, and many use blatant bait-and-switch tactics to lure in new customers. They court millions of uncreditworthy consumers every year, raising rates when the inevitable late and missed payments occur, and they seem oblivious to the fact that trying to collect on all that bad debt one day will be like getting blood from a stone. In 2009, the Federal Reserve reported that the United States holds nearly $2.5 trillion dollars in consumer debt, or $8,100 for each American citizen. This $8,100 does not include an individual's mortgage obligations; it is simply the amount of consumer debt. More specifically, the U.S. Census bureau reported that 173 million American citizens held credit cards as of 2006, and that number was projected to grow to 181 million by the end of 2010. These same Americans own approximately 1.5 billion cards—an average of nearly nine credit cards issued per card holder.*

## Fire in the Hole

When used carefully for its intended purpose, dynamite is a useful tool. But in the wrong hands, dynamite is a deadly hazard that can snuff out hundreds of lives in an instant. That's why I refer to credit cards as plastic dynamite—when a card is used with the proper restraint, it can be a useful tool for consumers. But when used without restraint, it takes a solid credit profile, built up carefully over time through hard work and sacrifice, and destroys it in the blink of an eye—and the collateral damage is enormous. It leads to having to dodge phone calls from collection agencies and the heavy emotional burden of being so deep in debt that you constantly worry if you'll ever get out from under. It puts unbearable stress on individuals and families and turns a comfortable or even prosperous existence into a living hell. I'm sure many of you reading this have found out the hard way what can happen when plastic dynamite suddenly explodes in our faces. And it's happening to thousands of people every day.

## Membership Had Its Privileges

You are no doubt familiar with those American Express commercials showing celebrity cardholders and the dates when they first opened their account ("Ella Fitzgerald—Member since 1982," for example). They talk about all of the wonderful advantages and conveniences of using an American Express card, and the idea behind the whole thing is that account holders may expect VIP treatment whenever they pull that card out of their wallets. In fact, the company slogan is, "Membership Has its Privileges"—you are a "member," not just an account holder. Owning an American Express card is like belonging to an exclusive club where everyone bends over backwards to cater to your needs. By putting the date the account was opened on the front of their cards, American Express implies that the longer you

---

* http://www.money-zine.com/Financial-Planning/Debt-Consolidation/
Consumer-Debt-Statistics/

own one, the better the service you could expect from them. Well, those days are gone.

The truth: You could be a member for 50 years, but if you fall behind on your payments, you're not going to get special treatment. Today's American Express is not about attracting new members; it's about alienating their old customers. They're cutting limits, raising rates, and have even offered cardholders $300 to close their accounts. It's like they're changing their slogan to "The American Express card—please leave home without it."

But don't single out just Amex. MasterCard, Visa, and all the rest are equally guilty of changing for the worse, as are the banks, like J.P. Morgan Chase, Citibank, Wells Fargo, and Bank of America, that back credit cards. Once upon a time, credit cards encouraged spending with rewards. They raised credit limits for their best long-term customers. Fixed rates stayed fixed. It was the Golden Age of credit cards—card issuers were happy, and their customers were happy. But where there's money involved, it's only a matter of time before greed starts to creep into the picture and spoil everything, and that's just what happened. Once they extended the privileges of membership to everyone, regardless of their financial circumstances, the stage was set for the collapse that has transformed the credit card industry into a wounded beast in survival mode.

Today, apart from the fact that meeting the eligibility requirements is suddenly a challenge, being the owner of a new credit card account is a much tougher proposition than before, with drastically lowered credit limits and huge rate hikes the norm. Yes, the credit card companies still reward you to spend, but with all the new loopholes they've added it's harder to collect on the reward. And let's face it; so-called reward points and miles are underused by cardholders and often are virtually useless. Since the recession hit starting in 2008, more people have been cashing in on their points to pay for travel, but for decades, huge amounts of spending-based points were never claimed. This is exactly what the credit card companies wanted and expected. Now, with shorter expiration dates on points and miles, it's easier than ever to forget to redeem points before they expire.

 Never assume your credit card terms and conditions won't change.

## Changing the Rules of the Game

Most credit cards are switched from fixed to variable rates, which means goodbye to the fixed rate that made having a credit card a manageable expense for so many. Grace periods are another casualty of the credit card industry's self-inflicted implosion, with interest accruing from day one in many cases. Credit limits have been lowered, even for the best customers with spotless credit histories. Then there's "credit chasing"—as soon as a cardholder pays down a portion of their balance, the credit card company proportionally lowers the cardholder's credit limit. This shrinks the cardholder's available credit, but even worse, it causes a drop in the cardholder's credit rating by reducing their credit capacity, which is driven by the amount of available credit on active cards. Knowing companies are doing this, cardholders also have a disincentive to pay down their balances.

Why is maintaining your credit capacity so important? Because it represents roughly 30 percent of your credit score. I explain more about credit capacity in Chapter 6, but to get an idea of how

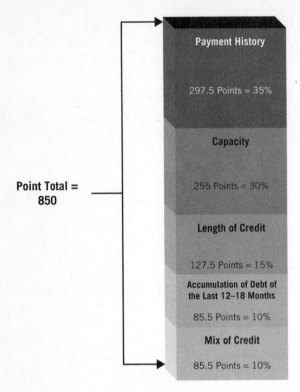

Figure 2.1    Credit Breakdown

vital your credit capacity is to your profile, take a look at this chart (Figure 2.1) showing the breakdown of factors credit bureaus consider when determining your score.

## The Gift That Keeps on Taking

People often take on new credit card debt with the attitude that if they can afford the resulting minimum monthly payment, they can afford the debt—a penny borrowed is a penny earned. Well, let me give you a great example of why this is nonsense. Susan and Mark came into my office for a loan. They had been married two months, and they were ready to buy their first home together.

911
SECRETS

Maxing out your credit cards will always result in a lower credit score.

While reviewing their financial history, I pointed to a brand new credit card that was at the max limit, and asked what it was. They looked at each other and laughed, and then Susan told me they had charged $5,000 on a credit card to pay for their honeymoon, figuring they could handle the debt by just paying the minimum each month. Their smiles faded when I did the math and told them at the rate they were going, their honeymoon, plus interest, would be paid off in full just in time for their 39th wedding anniversary. That was bad enough, but the damage it had already done to their credit score had forced them into a higher interest rate, pushing their projected monthly mortgage payments way above their budget. For Susan and Mark, the short-term decision to use a credit card to pay for something they really couldn't afford proved to be a huge mistake with long-term consequences.

## Someone Always Has It Worse Than You Do

Every day I hear credit horror stories, and one that stands out for me as an example of the financially deadly effects of unmanaged credit card debt was that of Ellen and Joe, a bright, successful couple earning over $150,000 a year. Ellen managed a telecom company, and was responsible for overseeing 70 employees; Joe worked as a nurse for Care Flight as a search and rescue team member, saving lives under dangerous conditions. They were a very dynamic and interesting couple, so I nearly fell out of my chair when I saw they had accumulated $246,000 in credit card debt. That meant they were making minimum monthly payments of $6,712. They had worked long, hard hours for years, their family had expanded, and now they needed a larger house. Even with their outstanding job stability and income this mountain of debt was fatal to their credit scores and any hope of financing for a new home.

Two hardworking people were denied their dream because of credit card mismanagement and the willingness of the credit card companies to allow them—even encourage them—to accumulate debt without regard for their ability to pay it off.

## Somebody Ought to Look into It . . .

The Credit Card Accountability, Responsibility, and Disclosure Act of 2009 was an attempt by Congress to rein in the unscrupulous behavior of the credit card companies. Among its provisions, the act bans unfair fee traps, required plain sight, plain language disclosures, deterred credit card company practices that have ensnared large numbers of unsuspecting, high-risk college students, and in general provided for greater accountability from the credit card companies. The act includes a fair payment allocation provision forcing credit card companies to pay down the highest rate first among a cardholder's multiple debt sources. So when a cardholder has charges accruing at 14.9 percent interest and cash advances accruing at 29.9 percent, the credit card company is required under this new law to use cardholder payments to pay down the cash advance balance first. It all sounds good, but it's too little and too late for millions of Americans swept up in the credit card free-for-all of recent years. The new law may help some people, but not enough and not for long, since the credit card industry never met a rule they couldn't get around or render obsolete by switching to a new tactic. All in all, I'd have to say it's better than nothing—but just barely.

## I'm Forever in Your Debt

Imagine that years ago, the banks that back credit cards realized their unfair practices would not be allowed to continue unchecked forever, so they decided to diversify their portfolio of deceptive products by introducing the debit card, even promoting it as a safe alternative to their own unsafe credit cards. Well, that's not exactly how it happened, but it might as well have, given the wolf in sheep's clothing that debit cards have become in recent years.

911 SECRETS

Debit cards were never designed to make your life easier. They were only designed to get as much of your money as possible.

Just like credit cards, debit cards started out as a mutually beneficial tool for banks and their customers. And just like credit cards, the presence of too much greed turned a useful tool into a conduit to siphon off more consumer income. There was a time when banks frowned on overdrafts, even though they made a modest fee when it happened, because they sought long-term profits associated with healthy, stable bank accounts. Then came the era of encouraging consumers to spend beyond their means in order to swell this year's profit margin, and then the banks shifted from promoting responsible banking to promoting any product that turned a profit, regardless of consequences.

Picture it: One day, some bank employee somewhere noticed the modest overdraft fee profits tucked away on the balance sheet, and decided it was an untapped resource. Soon, banks were pulling in billions of dollars a year on overdraft fees, partly through encouraging debit card overuse, and partly by deliberately pushing payment through on the larger purchases first, creating a domino effect of multiple overdrafts. And when I say "billions," I don't mean three or four billion; in 2009 alone, banks were estimated to have made $38 and $40 billion in overdraft fees. So much for the debit card—another useful tool when used responsibly, but not the foolproof alternative to credit cards the banks want us to think they are.

## Psst! How Would You Like to Save 10 Percent?

Department store credit cards, in my opinion, are financially hazardous no matter how careful you are. People open charge accounts with department stores and then buy things they didn't need or even want because the store offers them irresistible "discounts" for customers paying with a store charge. Stores even offer discounts for opening accounts at the time of purchase.

The next thing you know, somebody has overspent on a high-interest store charge card, and their credit gets whacked. It's what I call "the worst 10 percent you'll ever save." From the standpoint of trying to save your financial life, I would never recommend opening a store charge account. Being responsible for a credit card that can only be used in one store doesn't make any sense, given that these cards carry interest rates of 22 percent to 25 percent or more. I was in a department store not too long ago, and suddenly over the PA system I heard someone shout, "Jenny has three new accounts and is on her way to twelve!" The employees cheered. It turns out Jenny was a store employee who had convinced three shoppers to open a store charge account that day, and was shooting for 12 new accounts before closing so she could collect a modest commission. In my mind, that meant 12 more people with potential credit problems in a matter of minutes.

## The Rise of the One-Armed Bandit

Like all the other forms of plastic out there, the automated teller machine (ATM) began as a good idea. These days, many banks stay open late and even have Saturday hours, but years ago, if you didn't make it to the teller by 3:59 on a weekday, you simply went without cash until the banks reopened. The first ATMs were few and far between, but they were there in an emergency, and that was worth paying a transaction fee. More than 20 years later, the ATM is everywhere. There's one on the corner. There's one at the store. They're all over the place at sports stadiums and casinos. Any place where people spend money, you will find them. There are hundreds of thousands of them all over the planet—there are so many of them that if they all got up and started walking around, it would look like a massive invasion from outer space.

The problem with all that "convenience" is that, like a credit card, an ATM is a temptation to spend money you wouldn't otherwise think of spending. Even worse, the ATM has become yet another outlet for the banking industry's insatiable hunger for sources of profit created out of thin air—witness the "balance inquiry fee," the "fee for use of a non-bank ATM," and so on. The only benefit to be derived from using an ATM over a teller is that the ATM can't talk you into buying a bank product you don't want or need.

## The Rich Get Richer

I should mention prepaid gift cards, which are risk-free in terms of credit issues but are easily forgotten about and may expire before the recipient remembers to use it. Credit card companies love them for this reason, and who can blame them? They get their money up front and can count on a significant percentage of the cards expiring without being redeemed. That's literally giving money away, and to a multibillion-dollar business, no less.

This says a lot about consumer spending habits and attitudes about money, but it says even more about the ability of the credit industry to adapt their tactics to take maximum advantage of those habits and attitudes. The relationship between the credit card companies and their customers began as a creative form of financial assistance benefiting both sides, but clearly it has evolved into something closer to a parasite-host arrangement. And guess which party is the parasite?

The reality about credit, debit, and store cards is that they can only be used safely by a consumer who has researched and understands all the risks and only uses the cards in accordance with some very strict rules and restrictions. The overall theme of this book is to educate yourself about your credit and all the ways in which you can help or hurt it, because the more you know, the more empowered you'll become and the better equipped you will be to take control of your credit. The following list represents a how-to guide and safety manual for the use of cash alternatives.

1. *Read the fine print of your credit card agreement.* Find out if you are on a fixed or variable rate. As the name implies, fixed rates remain at a certain level, but variable rates invariably go up—never down. Ironically, under the new credit card rule I explained above, credit card companies can raise your rates faster than ever before, unless they are fixed. Unfortunately, with fixed rates becoming an endangered species, chances are your rate is variable.

2. *"Introductory" rate offers are usually teaser rates to lure you in.* These rates are very tempting, but before giving into temptation, you'd better know when the introductory rate period ends and how high it will go once it is over. I've seen introductory rates start as low as 1.99 percent and explode to over 34.9 percent when the introductory period ends.

3. *You might be paying interest from the date of purchase, even when you pay off the entire balance every month.* Many credit card companies start charging you interest on the day of purchase, but you can find a card that gives you a grace period of up to 25 days, which gives you the opportunity to pay off your balance in full with little or no interest accruing.

4. *You should never transfer your mortgage balance, car loan, or student loan to a credit card, regardless of how low the interest rate may appear.* You can be sure that something will eventually trigger a rate increase, and when that happens, that big chunk of transferred debt is going to overwhelm you.

5. *You need to shop your credit card "Terms and Conditions" every year.* Keep in mind that the interest rate is just part of your "Terms and Conditions." Also included are annual fees, grace periods, and minimum payments. Do your homework and you may be able to find a credit card company that will offer you a more competitive package of these three elements.

6. *Remember, you will never get what you are not willing to ask for.* Call your credit card company today and at least once a year. Ask them to lower your interest rates today. Also ask them to eliminate annual fees if they are being charged. Tell them that you will be shopping for a credit card company that is willing to do so if they are not. As long as you have a consistent positive payment history with that credit card company, this gives you leverage in asking for a better deal.

7. *Don't forget, minimum payment requirements vary, and many companies have recently made changes to their policies.* Check into how the minimum is calculated. The better you understand all of the factors involved, the better able you'll be to make smart choices.

8. *Avoid opening department store accounts; they can hurt your credit score.* You know how I feel about department store credit cards, but it bears repeating: Avoid the temptation of opening a department store credit card, especially when the benefit is an immediate "10 Percent Off Today's Purchase." The mistake in opening such an account is twofold. First, your credit score is going to drop because of where you are opening your account. A department store credit card is collected through a finance company, which is considered high-risk by the credit bureaus. Second, you have been persuaded into an impulse financial relationship when all you really went to the department store for was the item you had in mind. This is never a good idea.

9. *Make the right choice when considering which credit cards to pay off.* Choose the one that increases your monthly cash flow the most. In doing this, you create more capacity for yourself while increasing your cash flow to attack other debt. Keep in mind this is not always the credit card with the highest interest rate.

10. *Use the best ATM deal you can find.* Frequent ATM users need to locate a bank with a favorable ATM policy. This includes charging no fee for using the bank's ATMs, reimbursement

for incurring another bank's ATM fees, and free balance inquiries.

11. *Don't treat your debit card like a credit card.* When you use your debit card, make sure to record every transaction you or your other cardholders make in real time to avoid costly overdraft fees.

12. *Protect your balance when you use a debit card.* Always opt for the feature that rejects transactions when you have insufficient funds available. This way your $4 latte does not end up costing you $35.

13. *Get used to the idea of paying for everything with cash.* Make a trip to the bank when you need money, not just to avoid ATM fees, but to raise your awareness of the regular expenditures in your life. Physically going to the bank helps solidify the impression that money is actually flowing out of your account, as does watching the wad of bills you withdrew get smaller and smaller; charging is too painless and invisible to register with you. That piece of plastic in your pocket will make you far more likely to overspend, making cash a more realistic vehicle for buying things.

14. *Avoid cash advances; they are expensive and self-destructive.* Don't take cash advances on your cards, especially to pay off another debt—you're just making things worse. Cash advances are subject to much higher interest rates and fees, and will haunt you for years.

15. *Understand credit capacity.* I can't emphasize enough the importance of your credit capacity. Credit capacity is simply the ratio between your available credit, or limit, and the amount you've used. Credit capacity is covered in depth in Chapter 6. Using a log like the one shown in Table 2.1, calculate your credit capacity and keep track of it, because the credit bureaus are doing just that. This is not just an organizational tool; it's also a reality check on your debt that will influence your financial decision-making and help with the process of molding you into a conscious consumer.

**Table 2.1    Credit Capacity**

| Creditor | Interest Rate | Payment $ | Payment Due Date | Outstanding Bal. | Credit Limit | Capacity percent |
|---|---|---|---|---|---|---|
| Bank of America | 34.5 percent | $310 | | $3,529 | $3,500 | 101 percent |
| Target | 24.9 percent | $35 | | $201 | $200 | 101 percent |
| Citifinancial Retail | 22.9 percent | $90 | | $1,000 | $3,500 | 28 percent |
| Cap One | 22.9 percent | $51 | | $342 | $500 | 68 percent |
| Chase | 25.9 percent | $0 | | $0 | $400 | 0 percent |
| Citibank | 19.9 percent | $15 | | $100 | $300 | 33 percent |
| Cap One | 22.9 percent | $179 | | $4,443 | $5,000 | 89 percent |
| Sears | 22.9 percent | $14 | | $75 | $135 | 56 percent |
| **Total** | | $694 | | $9,690 | $13,535 | |

This chapter is intended to provide you with a better under-standing of how credit card companies and banks operate, how your credit score is affected by your credit card debt, and how marketers hired to sell risky credit products to you are working around the clock to stay one step ahead of restrictive legislation and anything else that stands between them and your money. It's hard to predict what they'll think of next, but consider recent developments like the "dormant account" fee, which is a charge for *not* using your card. Perhaps they'll figure out a way to assess a fee every time your card is removed from your wallet and exposed to oxygen. Whatever credit card companies come up with, they still have to draw you in, and

911 SECRETS

Closing your accounts and cutting up credit cards is the fastest way to kill your credit scores.

my goal is to strengthen your resistance to their overtures, help you stop the bleeding on any existing credit card debt, and give you the information you need to become an informed consumer—a marketer's worst nightmare.

With a smart approach to credit, those little rectangles of plastic dynamite you carry around can be handled without detonating. Credit cards are a reality in our lives and will continue to be for the foreseeable future, but we can at least make certain that we are choosing the best available credit product. There's a lot of detail involved, so it's important that you organize your credit card finances and have all the relevant information available at a glance. You can't turn back the clock to the good old days of credit cards, but you can make the best of the current environment by never allowing the credit card companies to catch you off guard again.

# Affairs of the Wallet: Marriage

My theme in this chapter is best summarized by the words of Isadora Duncan, who wrote in *My Life* (1927), "Any intelligent woman who reads the marriagestrange contract, and then goes into it, deserves all the consequences."

This is so true and it applies not only to women but to men as well. There is a tendency to romanticize the whole process. Prince Charming takes you away to live happily ever after, right? In over half of all cases, that simply never happens, and, in fact, entering a marriage without *full disclosure* is a disaster waiting to happen.

Never say "I do" without full disclosure; you are heading for a marriage full of trouble. Secrets are a big red flag.

## What You Need to Know before You Say I Do

By "full disclosure," I refer to the financial realm and not merely the romantic. A few basic ground rules for anyone thinking of getting married have to be followed just to protect your finances, credit rating, and future. So many "perfect" marriages are begun without this essential, logical, and rational step. It is not taken for several reasons:

1. *You don't want to threaten the romantic bubble.* An engagement can be one of the most romantic times of your life. It is probably going to be far more blissful than your marriage. I am not *only* a cynic about this; I know from experience and from the experiences of many clients that this is true. This romantic bubble can also act as a set of blinders placed over your eyes. Believe me, the romantic bubble is worth bursting if there are secrets revealed.

2. *You are afraid of what you might find.* Some people don't want to ask difficult questions because they are afraid they will be disillusioned. Your perfect mate might turn out to be a deadbeat, and then the whole marriage will be called off. This is an illogical but a common theme. Why would you want to marry a deadbeat? It could be that an otherwise nice person has some bad habits when it comes to how he handles money. Even worse, the undiscovered matters could be a symptom of a deeper character flaw. In either case, shouldn't you know the whole picture before you say "I do"?

3. *You are giving your "life partner" the benefit of the doubt.* Remember the corny line from the end of the book *Love Story*? "Love means never having to say you're sorry." The theme here was that if we love each other enough, everything can be forgiven. Is that really true? If you give someone else the benefit of the doubt, you are inviting disaster. This is not resolved only by asking your future spouse, "Is there anything in your financial past I should know about?" The problem with this question is that people don't always tell the truth. So go ahead and trust all you want, but also adopt the old Russian proverb: *Doverey no poverey* (trust but verify).

Demanding full disclosure is essential, but is it a deal breaker? I received the following e-mail from a client:

> Rodney—
>
> What is your advice for a newly engaged couple who are deciding on their future financial plans? My fiancé and I have reached a bump in the road on how much we will share with one another. He doesn't want to share information about his checking account until after we are married and I would like to see statements now.
>
> I can't convince him that it is the right thing to do now rather than later. Also he believes in maintaining a separate checking account and only transferring money into a joint account for paying bills, which would equate to me not having access to his separate account or having knowledge of what is going on with it.
>
> He and I are 30 and 31 respectively. I own a home, car is paid for, student loan debt from professional school and very small credit card debt (less than $1k). He has his own car, doesn't own any real property, is not financially responsible (evidenced by his credit report he allowed me to review), and has a small amount of student loan debt. I earn more income than he does, about $20k difference.
>
> Can we work though this or is this a deal breaker to our relationship?

This correspondence makes my point precisely. How important is that romantic bubble? Why won't the fiancé share information? And why should he be given the benefit of the doubt?

Why does he want to keep separate checking accounts? Why won't he tell his intended spouse about his financial situation? What is he hiding? Another way to approach this is to ask yourself, "If you are planning to get married, are secrecy and nondisclosure a good sign?" No. It is a deal breaker because it demonstrates that there is something very wrong here.

**911 SECRETS** You can tell a lot about people by what they tell you. Unfortunately, you find out more by what they don't tell you.

## Dating Interview Tips

Two people planning to spend their lives together can commit to full disclosure, and that is admirable when it happens. But this is not optional. Full disclosure is imperative. If a relationship starts out with secrets, you have to ask, "Why are we getting married?" Of course, some things are painful to discuss. There are, however, a few major issues beyond "I am not a virgin" or "I've been married before" or "I'm a transsexual." Some people think these are earth-shattering disclosures, but they could be minor compared to some of the possible financial issues that might not be disclosed, but should. For example:

- My credit score is low because I owe $50,000 in back child support (but my ex won't let me see the kids, so it's not my fault).
- I have lost two homes to foreclosure (however, I was a victim of predatory lending).
- I filed bankruptcy last year (that wasn't my fault either).
- My record includes a conviction for embezzlement (but it was all a big misunderstanding).
- I cosigned on my son's car and he's behind on the payments (but he's a crazy, mixed-up kid and I'm sure he'll fix the problem eventually).
- By the way, I can't open a bank account or buy property because I owe the Internal Revenue Service (IRS) $85,000 and there's a tax lien filed against me (but it's a conspiracy).

Disclosures should be made completely and without excuses. If you discover financial problems in your intended spouse's past, but

**911 SECRETS**

True love means never having to say "I forgot about that one little past problem."

each is accompanied by a set of excuses, it's a danger signal of the worst kind. It's a character flaw. Adults take responsibility for their mistakes, and don't repeat them or make up excuses. So a single error can be explained as a youthful indiscretion. But repetitive problems or excuses are not traits that are going to go away as soon as you say "I do." One unfortunate trait of many people is to believe that they will somehow change the other person. For women, it is a romantic notion that their love in and of itself will be enough to make a flawed person perfect. For men the equivalent idea is the "rescue syndrome." Some men think they are on a mission to rescue the damsel in distress by paying off her cosigned auto payment, tax lien, and past due credit cards, all as part of the marital deal. Big mistake.

You need to set a few basic standards for yourself and your "perfect" mate before agreeing to get married. First of all, full disclosure is not negotiable. This will include a complete and thorough mutual audit (explained in the next section) of each other's financial past. Part of that process should be that upon discovering that your intended has been deceptive, you should call off the wedding. No romantic notion should be strong enough for you to ignore the jeopardy you enter into when you hitch up with someone who does not want to tell you everything beforehand.

There are also variations of a con game to watch for in potential mates. It can be everything from immaturity or a past mistake, to lame explanations like "It's no big deal" or "I forgot about that," all the way to outright criminal fraud. In this situation, a person knowingly deceives and misleads you to get the meal ticket, or to take over your home and bank account and then disappear.

Being in love is the easiest state of mind for a con artist to exploit. The con man is an expert at knowing exactly what to say to make you forget your common sense. Don't allow yourself to be fooled.

**911 SECRETS** A con artist's easiest mark is a person in love.

The most revealing step you can take to protect yourself and to ensure that you are not making an expensive mistake is an exercise that I call the "dating interview." You have to ask a series of questions before committing to spend the rest of your life with the other person. I will give you a list of questions in the next section; but first I think it is important to remind you of a few logical red flags to look out for. You know these already, but when you think you're in love, you are not always thinking clearly. Here are some of the warning signs to look for during your dating interview:

1. *Anger.* If you bring up the topic of full disclosure and your "better half" reacts with anger, I think you'd better run in the other direction. An honest person is not going to get angry if you raise questions. In fact, an honest person will be encouraged that you are being so responsible, especially since the full disclosure is going to work in both directions. If someone has nothing to hide, there is nothing to get angry about.

2. *Indignation.* The indignant response is not quite the same as anger. With anger, the other person attacks you. But indignation is a self-righteous defense mechanism meant to shame you into backing down. "How dare you!" is one of the signs that you're dealing with a scoundrel. Watch out and keep one hand on your wallet.

3. *Evasiveness.* Some people will be puzzled or confused or display a lack of memory about past financial problems, or even come up with wild excuses like "all of my financial records were lost in a fire." Let's face it, we all know our own financial past, often with total recall. No one is going to forget what has happened to them, and lost records are easily replaced. An evasive response is another sign of deceptiveness.

4. *Distractions.* A con artist is like a magician; while you're watching one hand, the other hand is cupping a coin, hiding a card, or taking your wallet. Financial matters are dead-serious and not to be minimized. Someone who tries to use humor or changes the subject probably has a lot to hide, and they don't want you to find out what that is.

5. *Seduction.* This is the most difficult of all responses. "Come on, honey, talking about money stuff is boring. Wouldn't you rather have sex?"—a difficult one to pass up or resist. The appropriate response is to deal with the money stuff first and then have fun, or at the very least to make a firm appointment to get down to financial business. This is serious stuff, and it has to be dealt with as a priority, not put off or avoided through the use of seduction.

You start out your life together with responsible habits, too. A good way to judge the other person's ability to make a grown-up commitment is to propose a few rudimentary financial steps. These should include starting a savings and investment plan, preparing a financial budget, and realistically assessing your combined earning power. By the way, at this point, you also want to make sure that your prospective spouse is not intending to "retire" from his or her job right after the wedding. You probably need to have both incomes as you make plans to spend your lives together.

If the other person resists talking about these steps, it's a big problem. Why wouldn't you want to prepare a savings plan and family budget? These might not be fun, but they are necessary—not only because it helps you to identify potential monetary problems, but also because it focuses in on flaws in your goals. If your spouse expects to take expensive vacations, buy cars, or gamble away a big chunk of your income, you need to know that right now. Will you buy a house, have children, or take a vow of poverty and become third world missionaries? There are many important life decisions to make, and if your individual goals conflict, you are heading for trouble.

For example, just as a preliminary budgeting item, who is paying for your wedding? And how much is it going to cost? If you are going to be making payments yourself, do you have the money? If not, maybe you should consider a modest civil ceremony. It's not as romantic or memorable, but why go into debt at the very beginning of your marriage.

One hard and fast rule: *Never borrow money to pay for your wedding or honeymoon.*

**911 SECRETS** Starting out with debt is a poor beginning. If you can't afford to pay cash for your honeymoon—or convince your parents to pay for it—you're not ready to get married yet.

For many people, the demand for an expensive wedding and memorable honeymoon is more important than how it gets paid for. But it gets to the heart of my issue with people who don't have that important preliminary discussion: Why do you want to start out with a burden of debt? If you can't pay cash for these big events, you are not ready to get married. If your family isn't going to pay for the ceremony, you need to look for alternatives that cut costs, not alternatives that put you into debt.

## The Ten Steps You Must Take before Saying "I Do"

This is the difficult part: You have to make full disclosure, and demand the same from your intended spouse. If you take these steps, then you know what you're getting into because you have eliminated the unknown (or you know about disclosed problems, but proceed believing that "love conquers all"). Either way, knowing the facts is a requirement.

1. *Review both of your credit reports.* This seems like a basic step to take, but very few engaged people bother to take the simple step. For up to $15 you can quickly and thoroughly find out all you need to know about someone's credit history. Even giving the other person the benefit of the doubt, you at least have the chance to clear up and errors on your credit report at this phase.

His credit report will reveal if Mr. Right is also Mr. Financial Right.

You and your fiancé or fiancée should review both credit reports together. I am a firm believer that bad things happen to good people, but let's face it, some people are just irresponsible. If there are credit hurdles to overcome, you both need to know it going in. This is an opportunity to open up the lines of communication on a tough topic. What you really want to know is: What happened, why did it happen, and what can we do together to prevent it from happening again? I always hate to see that person on the TV talk show that had "no idea" what they were getting into when they married the wrong person. Many secrets would have been revealed if they had pulled a credit report up front.

2. *Check the credit reports for bankruptcies, tax liens, or judgments.* These are easily located on a credit report because they warrant their own section entitled "Public Records." Ideally, you'll see "Public Records" followed by the words "none

found." If you do find that either of your reports contains a public record, the warning sirens should sound, especially if this is the first you are hearing about it. These are not simply oversights or misunderstandings, but serious issues with long-lasting consequences. Millions of people have filed for bankruptcy protection, and it's not necessarily a reason for you to turn and run. It is, however, an event that warrants a good explanation. Many people experience bankruptcy as a result of job loss, divorce, medical issues, all of which may have been outside of their control. But some people live their financial lives on the edge, spend more than they make, and are one paycheck away from financial crisis. The sad truth is that many end up with multiple bankruptcies, because they didn't learn the first time. I'm not judging, I'm just saying you should know which one you're dealing with, and protect yourself accordingly.

**911 SECRETS**   To find the truth, you have to ask the tough questions.

I've heard it said that there's only two things that are guaranteed: death and taxes. But if your would-be spouse also owes back taxes, the debt will never simply go away, not even in bankruptcy. A tax lien attaches to property, garnishes wages, levies bank accounts, and wreaks havoc on your life. If your future spouse has a tax lien, marrying him or her can bring you under that lien. The first thing most couples do when they get married is open a joint checking account. If either party has a tax lien, the day will come—probably sooner than later—when your assets in that account will be frozen and then taken away, and no longer belong to you. If there's a tax lien, deal with it immediately. Settle it, set up a payment plan, whatever it takes, but remember, the IRS does not go away. A judgment is the most intense type of a collection. Judgments can be awarded on defaulted debts such as child support, apartment complexes, and auto repossessions—just to name a few. If a judgment shows on either report, you need to confront it and come up with an action plan. If you intend to buy a car financed with a decent rate, rent an apartment or home, or buy a home in your future, you need to get the judgment paid and released. I've seen judgments drop credit scores hundreds of points. It's a blemish you don't need and cannot afford.

3. *Review the past six months' credit card statements.* Look at the history of all of the cards, including activity during the holidays and any cards cancelled or paid off during the past year. Credit card statements hold the key to understanding each others' spending and buying habits, and they disclose whether either of you has been living beyond your means.

**911 SECRETS**

Always review your future spouse's spending habits. The numbers won't lie.

- Some signs to look out for: Over six months' worth of statements, note whether the balances are going up or down. If the balance increases each month, and only the minimum payments are being made, it's safe to say that the cardholder is spending more than he can afford to spend.
- Are there late fees? This is another warning sign of financial mismanagement. Are there any "over-limit fees?" You may want to start looking for the nearest exit at that point.
- Where are credit cards being used, and how often? Are they used to put gas, groceries or other day-to-day expenditures on a card, building balances at 19 percent interest?

Ideally you want to see charges being paid in full monthly, and balances going down each month—after all, your other half is getting ready to get married. Shouldn't they be trying to reduce debt versus adding to it? Take this opportunity to isolate and attack the problem together if there is one.

4. *Disclose any cosigned debts.* If your spouse to be is on the hook for someone else's debts, it can cause big problems later. I can't tell you the number of credit reports I've seen that are perfect, all except for one huge blemish. Inevitably, that blemish is a direct result of not being able to say "no." Let me explain. A son, daughter, boyfriend, girlfriend, etc. (you get the picture) wants to buy a car. They are unable to get approved for the financing, presumably because their credit or income isn't sufficient to carry the debt or because their credit report has too many late payments. Warning flag #1 flies at this point, but was missed. There's a reason they needed a cosigner. An agreement is made to cosign the debt with the "promise" that the primary signer will make all of the payments on time. Everyone has good intentions, and the relative has a new car. You have a new debt. What people fail to realize is that once you cosign, you own that debt. If the primary borrower doesn't make a payment, and you don't know about it, your credit is damaged as a result of the late payment. Even worse, if they stop making payments completely, you, as the cosigner, are directly responsible for making the payments. If the car gets repossessed, the creditor doesn't care if you were "just a cosigner," and your credit scores don't care either.

Cosigning for someone else is a nice gesture, assuming the other person makes all of the payments. That can be an expensive assumption.

I'll never forget the day that Andrew walked into my office. We had met months before, and I'd approved him for a loan to purchase a new home. He had been house hunting with his Realtor for about six months, and had placed an offer on a house. We sat down to update his file, and when I pulled his credit, my jaw dropped. "What's wrong?" he asked. I had to look him in the eye and tell him that his credit score had plummeted 246 points—wow. Suddenly, a look came across his face that told me he knew exactly what had happened. He was right. Right after our first meeting, Andrew met a woman who, he thought, was *the one.* He was so sure, and so in love that two weeks after meeting her, he cosigned for a brand-new car. He never thought twice, knowing that they would be together forever. Little did he know, she had a different plan. The permanent license plates hadn't even come in yet when she dumped him. Who was to blame really didn't matter. Now, here we were, and he was faced with repossession on his credit report, and no chance of obtaining a mortgage loan. I bring you this story to show that cosigning a debt is not an endeavor to take lightly. You'd better be willing and able to pay that debt should the other party not be able to do so. Even better advice, don't cosign for anyone. If you *must* cosign for a college-bound child who doesn't have sufficient credit, fine. But make sure the bills come to your address and have your child make payments directly to you. You then send the payments to the creditor. Your credit depends on it. Trust but verify.

5. *Decide whether you'll have a joint bank account, or each have your own individual account.* I recommend joint accounts, primarily because full disclosure is always the best way. Husband and wife both know what goes in and what goes out, and it's easier to stick to the household budget this way. However, there are many more opportunities for problems with a joint account. All it takes is one debit, ATM withdrawal or check that wasn't written down or disclosed, and the bounced check

madness ensues. A minor miscommunication or oversight can result in hundreds of dollars in fees. I'm not saying it can't happen on an individual account, but it's twice as likely to happen with two of you on the account. If you commit to communicate and balance the account together, a joint account is the way to go. If your new spouse has a history of mismanaging money (remember, you reviewed each others' last six months' credit card statements), individual accounts may be a safer alternative.

This raises an equally important question. If you want to go with individual accounts because your future spouse has a history of overdrafts and bounced checks, why are you still getting married? The problems are not going to be isolated to the joint checking account. These problems are *symptoms* of a broader lack of discipline and responsibility that is going to come up again and again throughout your marital history. Why do you want to invite problems like that? This fairly simple decision—joint or separate accounts—may lead you to question the whole premise that you *want* be get married.

6. *Elect a family chief financial officer (CFO).* This is the person who holds the checkbook and is going to be responsible for paying the bills each month. This should not be taken lightly, and there are many factors to consider when making the decision. Number one, who has the time to commit to managing the family business and budget? This is not a part-time job. The family CFO also needs to be organized. Nothing can stall a plan faster than a pile of bills on the counter mixed in with the kids' homework. Designate an office area from which to manage the household finances. This area should have an inbox for bills received, an area to keep grocery lists, coupons, and the family's budget log (see Figure 3.1).

Sounds easy, right? The truth is, much like holding a CFO designation in a big corporation, it's a tough job that requires a tough attitude. You may meet with some resistance from the

# Affairs of the Wallet: Marriage

| Monthly Bill Organizer | | | | |
|---|---|---|---|---|
| | Total Income This Month | Average Income Monthly | Due Date | Date Paid |
| **Monthly Income** | | | | |
| Your Income | | | | |
| Spouse Income | | | | |
| Total Income | $0.00 | $0.00 | | |
| **Monthly Bills** | Paid | Min Payment | | |
| Mortgage 1 | | | | |
| Mortgage 2 | | | | |
| Auto Loan 1 | | | | |
| Auto Loan 2 | | | | |
| Credit Card 1 | | | | |
| Credit Card 2 | | | | |
| Credit Card 3 | | | | |
| Student Loan 1 | | | | |
| Student Loan 2 | | | | |
| Personal Loan 1 | | | | |
| Day Care | | | | |
| Gas | | | | |
| Electric | | | | |
| Garbage | | | | |
| Water | | | | |
| Telephone/TV/Internet | | | | |
| Cell Phone | | | | |
| Auto Insurance | | | | |
| Life Insurance | | | | |
| Medical Insurance | | | | |
| Other | | | | |
| **Total Amounts** | | | | |
| *Total Amount of Bills Paid* | $0.00 | $0.00 | | |
| *Cash after Bills Paid* | $0.00 | $0.00 | | |

Figure 3.1   Monthly Bill Organizer

ranks when you make the tough decisions, such as getting rid of the movie channels to save $17 a month or recommending your spouse cut back on his or her spending habits. I'm not saying you have to be an obnoxious dictator—there is a balance here, but you also have to remember why you were elected—to save your family's financial life and make a better future for all of you.

**911 SECRETS**

Having a family CFO only works if both spouses follow the rules.

Many fiscal problems come up because neither person specifically took responsibility for these important matters. Worse still, what if you take responsibility but your spouse spends money behind your back? The budget is useless unless both sides agree to it, and you can find out a lot about your future spouse by his or her reaction when you propose a family budget and assigning the CFO. Most marital problems are rooted in disagreements about money; but you can spot emerging problems even before you enter the legal contract. Unless your prospective spouse is willing to agree to these basic necessities, your future marriage could already be doomed.

7.  *Set a budget.* Make it detailed enough to account for all of the income/outflow every month, including an emergency cash fund for unforeseen costs. Complete the budget log to show the minimum monthly expenses incurred in your household, and then look to see where any unnecessary funds are allocated. Don't reinvent the wheel right away. Make small, gradual changes over time versus denying yourself and your family all of the simple pleasures. The occasional dinner out or movie is crucial to your family's sanity, but just be conscious

about where you go and how often. The budget is much like a family's DNA—no two households are completely alike. The budget log is simply a tool to help get you started, and to see where your money goes.

A budget is not the *rule* for what you are going to spend. It is a measuring device to help you find financial flaws and fix them.

Creating your own log will prove to be both therapeutic and eye opening, and both spouses should be involved in this piece—let's face it, there may be debts that one hasn't exactly told the other about. This exercise will not work if there are any omissions, so a vow of honesty should be taken up front. All members of the family need to be made aware of the new budget and be willing to adhere to it. Once you have determined a specific monthly amount that will be saved, you'll need to determine if those funds are to be put into a savings account right away every month (an automatic savings deposit is a good idea), or if your family has debt, determine which debts will be paid off first. Celebrate every month that your savings grows and your debt decreases, and make a point of keeping track of progress monthly, every six months, and annually—just like a performance review. Remember, a "budget buster" will occur from time to time (car repairs, insurance deductibles, etc.). Be prepared, and don't let these minor setbacks discourage you. Life happens!

8. *Review health insurance cost and benefits.* In my research studies, over 40 percent of all credit reports I've reviewed have at least one medical collection on their credit report. This directly damages their credit scores. This small study is representative of all Americans' profiles from all walks of life.

I've seen medical collections as low as $1 drop a credit score by 120 points. This is one reason why a careful evaluation of your health care coverage is so important. You need to know what's covered, and what's not, as well as which hospitals and physicians are in network or out of network.

How does this relate to credit? Medical bills are the number one cause of bankruptcy. "Insurance should have covered that" is not recognized as a solution to remove a medical collection, yet it's the most common explanation that I hear. Here's the bottom line: If you receive a medical bill, you must confirm if you really owe it, and if you do, pay it or set up a payment arrangement. If you find that the insurance should cover it, get on the phone with the insurance company and confirm that they are paying it. It's your responsibility to be sure it ends up a zero balance account. The root of "healthy relationship" is health. As the cost of health care continues to skyrocket, so should the attention you pay to the options in your health care plan. If you are in a position where both of you are employed by companies that provide health benefits, consider yourself very fortunate. At least you have the option to choose between two health care plans to find the one that best suits your needs. The first consideration is to talk candidly about who feels better about their employment stability and the stability of the company overall. If your company is downsizing or you think that your job is in jeopardy, your partner's plan is probably the best option. If each of you has a job with a stable company, then compare each plan's coverage, monthly premium amounts, deductibles, copay for prescriptions and office visits, as well as the list of physicians on each plan. By making this simple comparison, the choice should become obvious. Don't ignore your deductibles and coverage, because when it's time to use the insurance, you'll quickly find out how much it can cost. Be sure you're prepared for a medical emergency, and have proper coverage for your family.

9. *If either of you has been previously married, review every page of the divorce decree(s).* As much as we hate to admit it, there's no way to enter into a new marriage without remnants of the old marriage bleeding into it. Reading a divorce decree doesn't have to be boring. Oh, the stories I could tell from the decrees I've reviewed over my 20 years in the lending business. It's amazing some of the things people will fight over and how long a bad decision can haunt a person. The divorce decree holds truths, secrets and long-term obligations that you need to know before you say "I do."

911 SECRETS    When it comes to credit, a divorce decree never releases you from financial liability.

The first thing to look for is the judge's signature, date of finalization, and the stamp of approval. A petition for divorce or temporary orders are not the same as a finalized divorce decree. As the saying goes, it ain't over until it's over. Once you've determined your prospective spouse is *really* divorced, look for any long-term resulting debts such as alimony and child support. These monthly payments need to be taken into consideration when establishing your new budget, and you need to know how many years remain. Although child support ends at 18 in many cases, sometimes it is much longer depending on the circumstances. For example, is your ex financially responsible for any future college tuition or student loans? While you're there, take this opportunity to confirm that the child support or alimony payments are current and are not delinquent. Next, look to see if there is any real estate owned and to whom it's awarded. There may be lump sums of money due to the ex that can wreak havoc on your honeymoon plans. If a marital household was awarded to one spouse or the other, be sure that the mortgage obligation has been addressed. Awarding the property does not release the other spouse of liability on the loan if it is a joint account, so the property should be sold or refinanced if at all possible. I've seen many credit situations arise as a result of an ex-spouse not paying a mortgage on time. Don't let the ex's irresponsibility sabotage your ability to buy a home later.

A true story that makes this point: Cindy is a long-time client of mine. I've provided two loans for her over a 10-year period. I'll never forget the first time she came into my office. A single woman with a great job, she bought her first home and received a good rate for the time—8 percent. A couple of years later, she came back to refinance when rates were considerably better. She had gotten married, but said that her husband had some bumps and bruises on his credit, so the plan was to do the refinance in her name alone. He would, however, be added to the title because Texas is a community property state. We completed the refinance at 6 percent with no problem.

A couple of years later, I received another call from Cindy. Rates were at an all time low, and I was able to offer Cindy a great rate at 4.25 percent with a lowered term to help her pay her home off faster. Everything looked great until I received the title commitment. My processor came into my office and said, "Rodney, we have a problem." Attached to the title of Cindy's home was a $54,000 judgment for back child support owed by her new husband. As a result, Cindy was unable to refinance her home. Not only that, but she could not sell her home without this judgment being satisfied. I called to advise Cindy of the problem, and could hear the devastation in her voice. She had no idea that this existed, and never even knew he was obligated to pay child support because his children were adults. Unfortunately, there was nothing I could do to change her situation. This is not as uncommon as one may think. It's a great example of why full disclosure up front is imperative.

10. *Check job history and stability of income.* These are key factors when determining if this person has staying power and the ability to simply hold down a job. If he or she changes jobs every three months, there might be a commitment issue on other levels as well. Ideally, a couple enters into marriage with a road map to financial success, and the biggest factor within that is income. We all know people who have embellished a résumé to get a job. There are even some who will embellish a résumé to get a great mate. Look, there are lots of "$30,000 millionaires"—these are the people who make $2,500 a month, and spend $5,000 a month, usually on credit cards. A résumé won't tell you everything, but when you compare it with the most recent three years' tax returns, the rest is revealed. It's simply a validation to support a person's reliability when it comes to maintaining a lifestyle. I'm not saying he or she needs to be rich, but let's face it: Money can't buy happiness, but it sure doesn't hurt.

Don't fool yourself about your financial situation. Being *rich* does not mean having a lot of credit, especially if your accounts are all maxed out. That's called being *poor.*

The job history and résumé reveal more about people than where they work and what skills they possess. It is also an attribute of *character* and anyone who exaggerates qualifications to get a job has a character flaw. Do you think someone like that—who would lie to an employer—might be just as likely to lie to a spouse? It's a question worth pondering.

The bottom line is this: Think with your head and not your heart. Ignoring the risk by purposefully not asking the right questions is simply inviting trouble. And believing that "love means never having to say you're sorry" or "love conquers all" is part of the delusional mystique or the romantic. Believe me, you will find very few romantics who have also succeeded financially. It's more likely that the successful person—who has managed to accumulate wealth *and* maintain a happy marriage—is more likely to be a pragmatist.

In the next chapter, I explore the equally important (and potentially *more* expensive) of the affairs of the wallet: divorce. Even if you are not yet married, you need to read this chapter so that you know what lies ahead if you don't perform your "relationship due diligence" today.

CHAPTER

# 4

# Affairs of the Wallet: Divorce

Divorce is a tough topic and a painful process. Statistics show that at least 50 percent of first marriages end in divorce, and 75 percent of all subsequent marriages meet the same fate. Let's face it, with statistics like that, most of us have either been through it or are likely to do so in the future. While no one *plans* on getting divorced, it's important to know how to protect yourself and your credit should it happen. These are the keys to coming out on the other side of divorce with your financial bearings and credit intact.

Any divorce has to include planning before the legal steps are taken, during the legal process, and even afterwards. You cannot just trust the legal system to completely dissolve a marriage, and you certainly cannot rely on your divorce attorney to protect your financial life. In one respect, the attorney serves only one purpose: knowing which papers to file with the court and walking you through the *legal* process of getting a signed "final" divorce decree. That attorney has no incentive to also counsel you on the related affairs of the wallet. In fact, I could even make the argument that the attorney's best interest includes keeping you in the dark. If and when troubles arise later, you are likely to hire the same attorney (for additional fees, of course) to help sort out the mess.

A divorce attorney will always ask for a retainer check and your financial statement. After that, you had better protect your financial life.

## What Your Spouse Might Turn Into

Why don't more people take steps to methodically and rationally avoid financial problems stemming from divorce? Financial unawareness is one reason, but even more is the mindset of a person going through a divorce. It is painful and stressful, and avoiding ugly confrontations or financial discussions is easier than dealing with them. People also go crazy when they get divorced. Be aware of the three types of people your spouse might become when you enter the divorce process. They might turn out to be:

1. *Hot to trot.* Even before the final decree is filed and signed, many a spouse goes through a "hot to trot" phase, seeking approval with new mates, and more. They may decide to seek the instant gratification of new clothes, a new car, even plastic surgery. Even though the time of a divorce (and immediately afterwards) are the *worst* times to splurge, many people want to compensate for the change, and they become financially and personally suicidal. Some even destroy their entire financial lives in the desire to "make up for lost time" or "find true love" or "vindicate" themselves for being treated badly.

2. *Anything you can do I can do better.* One-upmanship in divorce is one of the most expensive attributes and frankly, it is reckless behavior. The ex-husband buys a new sports car, so the ex-wife feels entitled to get herself an expensive vacation and a new wardrobe. Next thing you know, *both* are in debt up to their eyeballs. If you have ever seen this take place, you know there's nothing you can do but stand aside and watch the

self-destruction. This behavior leads to some bizarre acts—
selling a spouse's prized vintage auto for $100 to a local
dealer, taking out the chainsaw and dismantling the entire
house, and more acts far more expensive and destructive
than just tearing up someone's clothes or throwing their personal possessions out onto the driveway. The "anything you
can do I can do better" behavior is invariably destructive to
both sides.

3. *Woe is me.* The third type of ex is the *victim.* These are the people who stay inside alone crying or eating excessively, or who
spend a fortune on therapy, or who get so depressed they lose
their job, stop paying their bills, and convince themselves that
their life no longer has meaning. That is giving a lot of power
to the ex and often is also very manipulative. It almost never
works and usually leads to friends and family viewing them as
pathetic rather than generating sympathy.

All three of these types have one thing in common: They spur
the economy quite directly through their acting out during the
divorce process. Because half of all first marriages end, it means
someone is going to be moving out. In addition to the cost of moving, this means that one home or apartment is replaced with two;
one set of furniture is augmented with new purchases; and one
family car becomes one family car each. It's not just the attorneys'
fees that are financially destructive during a divorce, but the costs
of moving, starting over, and simply having to spend money. The
new expenses you cannot avoid may be the least of your problems if
your divorce is coupled with an expensive makeover, mid-life crises,
or the exercise of newfound freedom.

But isn't the financial question supposed to be taken care of by
your attorney? Doesn't the divorce attorney give you advice about
how much you can spend? Of course not. Even the basics like who
gets what and who is on the hook for which debts *should* be part of
the process, but often they are not. Shouldn't your attorney have
diligently taken care of the financial angles as part of your divorce?

Logically, perhaps. But legally, the attorney is under no obligation to protect you from the financial pitfalls.

## I Thought I Was Divorced

You might view divorce as a static event that has a beginning and an end. Before the divorce, you were married and after the divorce, you are single, right? Wrong. Unless you take steps to ensure that your divorce includes a complete *financial* separation, you could end up as an unwilling lifelong cosigner with your ex.

Just because a divorce is "finalized" does not mean it's over. Many times, it's far from over, and your credit can be destroyed in the ongoing battles. The key is preparation, foresight, and good counsel. Amicable or not, divorce is nasty business, and you must be prepared for anything. Later on in this chapter, I present you with a checklist of 15 things you *must* do before filing that divorce petition. Joint debts incurred during your marriage are truly the ties that bind, and a divorce decree does not release you from liability. That stack of paper will not protect your credit from damage and plummeting credit scores.

As a starting point in the divorce process, how do you pick the "right" attorney? This is not as easy as it sounds. Divorce is a stressful, painful, and tragic condition, and both husband and wife go through periods of grief and anger during their divorce. Most people want to get away from this negative environment as soon as possible. In some cases, it's almost as bad as grieving the death of a loved one if, for no other reason, the topic of your grief—a failed marriage—is alive and well in the other spouse while the process goes on.

So how do you find an attorney who knows the law and who respects you for what you are going through? The best candidate is someone who also knows how *financial* law works. A lawyer who will handle divorce is most valuable if he or she also takes on cases involving real estate, probate, estate planning, bankruptcy, and similar matters. This attorney is going to be more of a Renaissance man (or woman) respecting the intricacies of property settlement, child support, real estate, and retirement accounts—in other words, the financial aspects of divorce.

Where do you find this versatile and experienced attorney? Forget about referrals from your divorced friends. They are more likely to refer you to their ex's lawyer than to their own. Most people who have been through a divorce using the exploitive "family law" practitioner think they got a raw deal, not realizing that their ex probably had the same kind of experience. You should retain a lawyer based on recommendation, but that should come from professionals you already use: your banker, real estate broker, accountant, financial planner, or the attorney you use for other matters. In asking for a referral, be sure you clarify that you need someone with financial sophistication, and not just someone who knows how to file the paperwork. If that was all that was involved with divorce, everyone could do their own without hiring a lawyer.

An easy test to apply in deciding whether or not to hire an attorney is to ask about how to protect yourself against future financial problems. If the attorney has no idea what you're talking about or brushes off your concerns, what does that mean? For example, he or she says: "Divorced is divorced. Once I file the paperwork, it's over." This means the person is not qualified to provide you with a long-term financial defensive plan to get through your divorce legally *and* financially. Even your uncontested, do-it-yourself fast and easy divorce is not going to include provisions for avoiding the nightmare that many divorced people go through later.

## Horror Stories

Robert had seen some curve balls in his life, but when he came in to get preapproved to purchase a home, he got a surprise like none he'd ever experienced. Robert had been married for 15 years, and had gone through an ugly divorce the year prior. He painstakingly rebuilt his life, and thought that his divorce was behind him. When we reviewed his credit together, a truly devastating reality hit him.

There was a mortgage on his credit report from the home he lost in his divorce. The Judge had awarded the home to his ex-wife, and Robert had moved out and been renting for over a year now. What he didn't know is that the joint mortgage stayed on his credit report, and his wife had not been paying the debt in a timely manner. Over the past year, she had made payments 30 and 60 days late consistently, and, although the decree said it was her responsibility, his credit scores were impacted significantly. So significantly, in fact, that I couldn't obtain a mortgage loan approval for him. Even after a year on his own, his credit was haunted by her actions.

**911 SECRETS** Know the difference between being divorced and being financially divorced.

I am cautioning you that a final decree of divorce does not mean your marriage is over and done with. You have to rely on careful preparation *before* filing for divorce, negotiation with your spouse on matters like child support or alimony, if applicable, and the property settlement. None of these are easy, and even the best attorney can only do so much.

After your divorce is finalized, even if your ex keeps up payments but is late a few times, that can be devastating. One of the first questions a future mortgage lender is going to want answered is, *Have you ever been late on a house payment?* You might not be, but if your ex is late and your name is still on the paperwork, that goes against you. In the credit world, your ex making a late payment means that *you* have also been late on a mortgage payment. You might be able to explain your way out of it, assuming you get the chance. It's more likely that your application will be rejected without a specific explanation. Have you ever seen the blanket statement lenders give you as a reason for rejecting your loan?

We are sorry to inform you that your application has been denied. This decision was based on a review of your credit history, during which we concluded:

- excessive number of outstanding credit cards and outstanding balances
- late payments on existing debt obligations

This blanket statement may include any number of issues, including your own late payments or an ex's problems on debts held jointly during your marriage. It can include mortgages, credit cards, and revolving credit accounts.

Even if you are diligent in negotiating a property settlement, that should include assignment of existing debts. With so much emphasis on "who gets what," it is easy to overlook the other side of the issue: "who *owes* what?" What if your divorce attorney friend overlooks a significant debt and it doesn't get assigned in the paperwork? Just a few months ago, I was having lunch with an attorney friend, and our conversation turned to business. I casually mentioned that our businesses were very closely tied. "How so?" he asked, intrigued by my statement. I went on to tell him how many clients come in to my office every year whose credit reports are destroyed as a result of a divorce. It's not the divorce itself that devastates the client's credit; it's more specifically what the attorney failed to do for the client. Couples establish "joint" credit accounts over their years of marriage. At the time a divorce is imminent, and the attorney is contacted, the credit obligations may be discussed, but don't get into the detail necessary to protect the client. I explained to him that, when the judge awards a joint account to one of the parties, it does *not* release the other party of liability. Husband thinks the account was awarded to wife, and he is consumed by a false sense of security—he thinks that he's no longer responsible. The reality is this—if she doesn't pay the debt, it still reports on his credit, he's still responsible, and the debt can haunt him forever. The attorney admitted that he had never thought of that, and was unaware that this was happening. After our discussion, he committed to change his procedure to require a joint credit report to be reviewed at the first meeting. He would go through line by line, and advise his clients to pay off and close all joint accounts immediately to protect their future credit rating. He also would be sure to outline the debts awarded in the decree, using the credit report as a guide to ensure no debts were inadvertently missed.

**911 SECRETS** Ignoring financial obligations will always lower your credit score.

Making matters worse, what if neither you nor your spouse takes responsibility for the debt, but simply assumes it is the other one's problem? First of all, you probably don't have recourse against the attorney even if he or she was clearly negligent. Second, in this situation, the law creates a huge pit for you to fall into. It is no longer a matter of "joint responsibility" for a debt, but becomes "either one's responsibility." This means the holder of the debt—the lender—can and will demand payment from either of you, and is most likely to look for the deepest pockets. Meanwhile, even if you are not morally obligated to the debt, your credit is going to suffer. A default or late payment is a huge negative on your credit report; and in this situation, you have no legitimate argument for removing the stain from your credit. It *is* your legal obligation.

A diligent attorney should (and a few do) run credit checks on both spouses, determine *all* of the debts involved, and insist that all be negotiated and assigned. The attorney should also insist—as part of the property settlement—that the person to whom a debt is assigned renegotiate the debt with the lender. Few lenders are going to simply take your name off a debt obligation just because you get divorced. You are going to need to insist on refinancing the debt on a home assigned to your ex, even if that means having to refinance the home for cash-out and consolidation. You will need to *insist* because, by law, a judge can require a refinance in the decree but can't enforce it. You also are going to need to make sure all jointly held credit cards are canceled and replaced. In some cases, if a credit card is issued in your name only and you just asked for a second card in your ex's name, the company might remove that name. But if you are joint card holders, you are going to have to cancel the card, negotiate responsibility for repayment, and take steps to ensure that your ex abides by the agreement. Even if a joint account is canceled, the debt still has to be repaid; and if your ex agrees to pay off the balances and then fails to do so (or is late on making payments) that still goes against your credit.

So, how do you avoid these problems? First of all, you need to recognize that divorce is not simply a matter of static process within the legal system. It involves potentially ongoing financial obligations on both sides in a perverse system where you can be held responsible for your ex's irresponsible habits. Given the kinds of things vindictive exes have been known to do, it is conceivable that a spouse may even intentionally destroy your credit by making late payments. That may be suicidal for the ex's credit, but for some exes, vengeance is illogical.

Identity theft is a major problem in our society. It's true that identity thieves can obtain enough information to open accounts in complete strangers' names, steal their credit and their money, and leave a path of destruction a mile wide for innocent people to try and clean up. If strangers can do it, imagine how easy it is for someone who knows *everything* about you. Divorce brings out the worst in people, and when there are feelings of betrayal and anger, ruthless vindication can ensue. Lisa was a woman scorned. She felt that her husband had betrayed her, and that the best revenge would be via his pocketbook. She opened three new credit cards in *his* name, and proceeded to shop with reckless abandon. Matt didn't know about the new cards until he applied to refinance the house into his name after the divorce was finalized. Imagine his surprise when he had over $30,000 in brand-new credit card debt, and of course, late payments on all three accounts because she had no intention of paying the debts. Matt had three options, the first of which would be to file a police report against her; however, this isn't an easy choice. Matt and Lisa have three children, and Lisa had custody of the kids. Sending her to jail was not an option. Option 2 would be to simply pay and close the debts, but the divorce had left him broke already. Option 3 was to get the debts caught up and pay the monthly minimums to try and salvage his credit. Of course, he should put a fraud alert on his credit report and pay for a monitoring company to protect himself in the future. Lastly, if none of these three options were possible, he could end up in bankruptcy as a last resort.

You need to understand that an angry divorce is likely to be characterized by an ex using whatever weapons are available. Among the most tragic is the corruption of a child's affections as a form of vengeance for a divorce. This usually occurs when the custodial parent poisons a child's mind to believe that the other spouse is evil. "He left because he doesn't love you anymore" is not untypical of the kinds of statements made to destroy the relationship between a parent and a child. It is not only tragic; it is a form of extreme child abuse, but it is common. An expert named Dr. Richard Gardner coined the term *parental alienation syndrome*. He explained that a child never recovers, even after realizing what was done to him or her. It becomes a lifelong scar of guilt.

Parental alienation syndrome is a tragic and cruel matter. But perhaps equally devastating is what I call *financial* alienation syndrome, the ongoing problems created when property is appropriated between spouses but the obligation remains undefined or continues to be held jointly. This problem is one of many reasons that you need to work with an attorney who is financially aware and sophisticated enough to protect you against this financial alienation. The symptoms of the syndrome include three parts:

1. Obligation without control
2. A declining credit score coupled with an inability to fix the problem
3. Inability to reverse the problem without added financial expense

In addition to using the most qualified attorney with both family law and financial experience, you also need to take 15 specific steps *before* you file for divorce. These steps are critical if you want to avoid losing control over your credit and the security of your financial health.

## The 15 Steps You Need to Take First

Below are the 15 steps everyone going through a divorce should take. I estimate that most people in this situation take at most only two or three of these steps. But all 15 are crucial, and failing to take action creates a direct threat to your financial security and your credit rating.

1. *Change your address.* Everyone knows that someone is going to move when a divorce happens. In the stress of this change, however, you have to methodically make sure that you actually file a "change of address" notification with your post office *and* also notify all of your creditors, utility companies, doctors, and others about where to send your bills. If you don't have a permanent address yet, set up a box at the local UPS store or FedEx/Kinko's. For about $120 per year, you can create a permanent address, and delaying this step can be expensive. Many times in a separation and divorce, multiple moves have to be made until you settle in a permanent home.

You may be sleeping on a friend's couch for a couple of months while you decide your next move, but that friend doesn't necessarily want to get your mail for the next six months. For some reason, those little yellow forwarding address stickers do not always find you—take the proper precautions to ensure all of your mail gets delivered to you, with your privacy intact.

Creditors and collection agencies are not going to put out an All Points Bulletin for you. If you move, it's your responsibility to advise every one of them of your forwarding address. In the old days of credit, if a collection or late payment showed up on your credit report, you could simply provide a letter, and it could be explained away. Times have changed. Your credit scores don't accept excuses. If you leave and the ex is getting the mail, what's to keep him or her from shredding it? You may miss a payment to a creditor, and *bam*—a credit blemish appears.

2. *Get a joint credit report before visiting your attorney.* It is imperative that you have an accurate assessment of your (and your spouse's) credit life. There may be accounts you didn't even know existed, and could be stuck with as a result. Pull the report and study it. This is the only way to make sure that you don't have to contend later with unknown joint debts.

3. *Itemize existing balances and monthly payments.* Know what's owed and to whom. Know which accounts are held individually and which are joint accounts (both of you are equally obligated to pay on a joint account). (See Table 4.1.)

**Table 4.1  Identifying Credit Obligations**

| Creditor | Balance | Payment | His | Hers | Joint |
|---|---|---|---|---|---|
| Ford Motor Credit | $20,000.00 | $455.00 | | | √ |
| Discover | $8,362.63 | $243.00 | | | √ |
| Sallie Mae | $6,535.61 | $80.54 | √ | | |
| Kohl's | $328.79 | $15.00 | | √ | |

4. *Know what you want.* Determine which debts you are willing to take responsibility to pay, and which debts you want to go to your ex-spouse. I strongly suggest that any accounts held individually stay with that person. The last thing you want is your ex controlling your credit future.

5. *Pay off and close all joint accounts.* Remember, just because the decree awards a joint account to one person, it does not have the power to release the other of liability.

6. *Be sure the petition for divorce itemizes every debt owed and cross-reference with the joint credit report.* The divorce petition and decree must show the creditor's name, full account number, any security tied to the debt (i.e., property address for a mortgage, vehicle identification number (VIN) for an auto loan, and so forth). Surprisingly, many attorneys either do not know this or simply don't bother to add in all of the details.

   Each debt must be awarded as the responsibility of one spouse or the other. Your attorney is not a credit expert, and while many people have faith that he or she has all of the knowledge necessary to protect you, most times that's not the case. Divorce attorneys know a lot about the law, but don't necessarily know anything about credit.

7. *Call all creditors on the credit report to ensure they have your contact information to notify you in case any debts go delinquent.* Anyone who has ever missed a payment knows the creditor will call as many numbers as they have on file to encourage a payment to be made.

8. *Invest in a credit monitoring program from the date of separation forward.* While you're distracted by the emotional turmoil of divorce, your creditors are still waiting patiently for you to make a mistake. A good credit monitoring system should cost you about $100 a year, but can save you so much more.

9. *Monitor credit card balances every day from the date of separation forward.* I can't tell you how many people I've seen get blindsided by the estranged spouse's shopping spree. And the often-required temporary restraining order (TRO) designed to

prevent either side from emptying accounts, is really entirely ineffective at preventing a buying spree or hiding assets.

10. *Check joint bank account balances daily.* With both sides having equal access to the account and strained communication at best, let's face it, balancing a checkbook is next to impossible. Checks written to *two* attorneys, new debts associated with the separation (apartment deposits, utility startup, etc.)—the list goes on and on. Many times the judge may have ordered this account to remain open, which makes no sense financially, but is intended to prevent one or the other from opening new accounts and hiding funds.

11. *Change your ATM and credit card PIN numbers on all accounts.* Remember, all of these are *joint* accounts. So even with that TRO is place, a vindictive spouse can empty out your account or max out your credit card. The worst situation is one in which you have already agreed to take on the obligation for a credit card, without knowing your spouse has already run up the balance. So make those changes right away.

12. *Open an individual bank account.* This is sensible and necessary just to protect you from the complexity of how to deal with joint accounts during and after the divorce. This makes sense, but so many divorcing people don't take this easy step. Do it right away. If a judge later tells you to keep the existing joint account open, make sure that there is little money in there, and also demand that once the final decree has been filed, all joint accounts be closed.

13. *Set up direct deposits and auto drafts to your new individual bank account—remove them from the joint account as soon as possible.* Today, many families have set up easy direct deposit for their paychecks, as well as many monthly payments. All of these must be changed at once. For obligations you are going to keep, move automatic payments so that they come from your newly established individual account. And please, please, make sure your employer does not continue to deposit your paycheck into the joint account.

14. *Put a fraud alert on your credit report.* Don't fall into the trap of telling yourself your spouse "would never open an account in my name without telling me." That person you once admired as ethical and honest might turn out to be a completely different person when you're going through a divorce. And remember, your spouse has all of the essential information they need: Your name, social security number, date or birth and mother's maiden name. If they set up accounts with statements going to their address and not to yours, then you are going to have huge problems.

    Although this is a rather obvious form of identity theft, before your divorce is final you are in a legal limbo of sorts. How can spouses steal the identity of the people they are married to, and who share joint ownership of accounts? On a legal basis, this is an ugly possibility, and you have to take steps before problems occur, to make sure no one can open an account using your private information.

15. *Control your situation.* Don't allow your emotions to get in the way of doing what's right to protect your credit and financial stability. Don't be afraid of being accused of acting ruthlessly or selfishly. By definition, divorce requires defensive steps. Amicable or not, divorce can ruin your financial life—don't let it.

A divorce, even in the best of circumstances, is going to be painful and difficult. You can help to ease a lot of the pain by remembering that a "final" divorce is not the same as a final *financial* divorce. You need to make absolutely certain that you have severed all of your financial ties to your ex to avoid nasty surprises in the future. For this reason alone, you cannot settle for an attorney who practices only in family law. You need an experienced attorney who also knows all about financial issues, including real estate, tax law, retirement planning, and financial planning. If you are going through a divorce, start by memorizing the 15 steps above, and using these as your guide for protecting your interests now and in the future.

# CHAPTER 5

# Collections: Deal with It

It's the reverse 911 call that can change your life, but it's also one of the hardest calls people answer. People may avoid picking up the phone when they know who's on the other end—the bill collector looking for money owed. It causes problems at work and at home, and it makes life a living hell. The devil you made won't go away and must be dealt with now. You have to pick up the phone; a solution is probably a lot closer than you think.

In the credit world, once a company has exhausted its attempts to get timely payment, they turn to *collections,* the process of trying to settle debts through direct appeal, garnishment, or legal action. Don't fall for the myth of believing that credit card companies "enjoy" turning an account over for collection. Once that step is taken, they get only a fraction—pennies on the dollar—if anything. It is a last resort.

It's ironic that many people are so resentful of their lenders (mortgage lenders, credit card companies, finance companies) that they become *self*-destructive. A dispute over whether or not you owe the debt itself should not be resolved by cutting off communication or by automatically allowing the account to go to collection. Once that happens, your credit rating will fall precipitously, and it will take years to recover. Meanwhile, you might not get that mortgage loan you need. Poor credit may even affect your ability to get a better job.

## Stop Being Right

I want to share a personal story that illustrates how even a small collection problem can mushroom into a disastrous one. In 1998 I had been divorced for five years and had not even lived in Arizona where my ex resided, for that whole time. Later on, when rates began to drop and refinancing seemed beneficial, I pulled my credit report to assess my options. Imagine my shock when there were two past due items that had gone to collection, both from Arizona. One was $300 for a cable box my ex had not returned to the company when service stopped and the other was $62 for the final cable bill. The service had been in my name, which was why these past due charges showed up on my report. I had overlooked the importance of getting those out of my name. This mistake had taken my credit score from 790 down to 632.

I had three choices. I could have been "right" and stubbornly refused to pay these charges. After all, they really belonged to my ex—not to me. But losing out on the opportunity to refinance would have cost me $350 per month in extra interest, $4,200 per year, and $21,000 over five years. Extending that out for a 30-year mortgage, the cost of "being right" would potentially cost me $126,000, originating from a $362 collection.

Rationally, refusing to pay the bill would be financial suicide, but I completely understand why many people make this choice, even years after a divorce. Upon discovering issues like this, it brings up all of the past anger. Doing nothing would have satisfied my "need to be right," but it would have been an expensive choice.

A second choice would have been to just pay the charges and be done with it—but would I be done with it? Once you pay off charges showing up as past due, you will find it next to impossible to get them removed from your credit report. For this reason, I took the third—and best—choice available. I negotiated.

*Before* you pay off the charges, you must negotiate removal of the negative item from your credit report, to take place as soon as you make the payment. Get this in writing. Don't trust the word of an anonymous clerk you talk to on the phone. Your letter should promise to immediately remove the delinquent mark upon payment of the entire bill. I made this deal, paid the $362, and cleaned up my credit reports. Eventually, I was able to get my refinance and lower my monthly mortgage payments. My own experience makes an important point: You can be right, literally, and still suffer due to a stubborn insistence that you are not going to pay a bill. Many a righteous person has gone to the financial gallows for this position.

What about those cases in which a negative item (like a delinquent payment or an outstanding account) you've never even heard of shows up? If you are not even sure you owe the money or were late on the payment, don't shrug it off. Take three verification steps right away:

1. *Original creditor.* If you do not recognize the name of the creditor on your credit report, inquire further. It is not always easy. For example, you might have applied for a credit card with a bank listed, but on the credit report a different organization shows up, a bank holding company, for example. So the identity of the creditor is not always going to be obvious. If the account has gone to a collection agency, you will need to phone that agency to get the information you need. The agency has every incentive to provide you with the name because they only make money if you pay up.

2. *Total amount owed as well as accumulated penalties and interest.* In your inquiry, whether with the original lender or a collection agency, ask for an itemized summary of the original debt and accumulated interest and penalties. Companies may be willing to discharge the debt and remove the negative item from your credit report even after negotiating with you. For example, you may offer to pay the original debt immediately in exchange for forgiveness of the interest and penalties.

**3.** *Original date the account went to collection.* Once an account goes to collection, negotiation to reduce interest and penalties accumulated prior to that time becomes more difficult. While the original creditor can negotiate a partial settlement with you, the collection agency has less incentive. They get a percentage based on what they collect. With this in mind, determine the exact date the original creditor sent the debt to collection, and then see if that collection agency will be willing to reduce the debt for interest and fees up to that point. In any event, you need to make sure that the negative item will be removed from your credit report in exchange for a negotiated payment plan. You have to ensure that the negative item is going to be *removed* completely. It is not enough to have it labeled as "paid" or "settled" because that does not fix the problem.

## The Truth about the Seven-Year Rule

Most people have heard that a negative item remains on a credit report for seven years, then falls off. If you insist on being right and you think you can suffer through seven years of poor credit, it could be worthwhile to avoid collections and refuse to pay—right? Wrong. The seven-year rule is not quite that simple.

 The key to the seven-year rule is knowing when the clock starts and restarts.

Some people play a little game of cat-and-mouse with their debts, opening bank accounts in other people's name and taking jobs that pay cash under the table. Disappearing from the credit radar can be done, but it is not easy and ends up costing you more money than it saves. Think about it. You can't even win the lottery without creditors showing up and demanding a piece of the action.

The seven-year rule is essentially a statute of limitations on an outstanding debt. After seven years have elapsed, the debt should theoretically disappear. However, you should know which debts fall under this rule and which ones do not. Debts that should disappear after seven years include tax liens you have paid, accounts assigned to a collection agency or written off as a bad debt, and any delinquencies or debts that are older than seven years. Some information, such as bankruptcy, remains on your credit report for 10 years. A separate rule applies to judgments filed against you as the result of lawsuits; that information remains for either seven and a half years or until the legal statute of limitations on the judgment has passed, whichever is longer.

The seven-year mark begins from the first date the status is changed to a collection account. However, some people believe a debt can be re-aged, meaning the seven-year clock begins to tick all over again if the account is assigned to an additional collection agency. A debt collector cannot legally re-age a debt; to do so would violate two federal laws, the Fair Debt Collections Practices Act and the Fair Credit Reporting Act. If you discover that a debt has been re-aged, you have to immediately dispute it and cite these two laws that the practice violates.

If you are inclined to play cat-and-mouse with a collection agency, keep in mind that once the debt is finally written off, it may be reported to the IRS and may become taxable income to you. Even if you can prevent creditors and collection agencies from finding you, the IRS is not as easy to deceive. It *will* find you, and it *will* collect the taxes you owe.

## Your Action Plan

In addition to monitoring your credit reports from all three agencies and taking immediate steps to remove collections past seven years old, you need to manage collection debts by asking yourself three important questions:

1. *Am I willing to pay this debt?* Depending on the nature of the debt, its origin, and (of course) the amount, you have to begin with this simple but important question. Small debts affect your score just as negatively as large debts; literally, a $5 collection can effect you just as much as a $5,000 collection. If you are able, pay off balances that are under a few hundred dollars and clean up your credit. Minimizing the number of delinquencies and disputes on your report is ideal. The way creditors see these types of derogatory items is that while one or two might have a reasonable explanation, having multiple collections reveals a pattern of problems and becomes more of a character issue. Sure, it's always someone else's fault, as the explanations might go. Realistically, why would anyone have a string of delinquencies, one after the other? You need to clean up your credit report to eliminate as many negative items as possible.

2. *Am I willing to settle this debt?* Paying off the entire amount is only one option. You can also make an offer to settle the debt for part of the total. This can include forgiving late fees and interest, for example. A creditor is often willing to waive these fees if it means getting the original debt. If it is a large debt and you simply cannot afford the whole amount, you can also negotiate a reduced payment. The creditor might accept a settlement, depending on the amount, the age of the debt, and—most important of all—how much cooperation you are displaying. If you are sincere, the creditor is always going to be more likely to work with you and to compromise. If you play games or don't keep your promises, the trust goes out the window.

3. *Am I willing to set up a repayment plan?* If you want to make a series of payments according to a schedule, remember these provisions: First, as part of the agreement, the creditor should

cease adding additional fees or interest. Second, don't miss any payments, as that immediately cancels the whole deal. Third, make sure that as part of the amended contract, once the agreed-upon debt has been satisfied, the creditor will immediately remove the negative item from your credit report and show the debt paid in full.

**911 SECRETS** There are no short-cuts to fixing poor credit. You are going to need to pay, settle, or set up a repayment plan to undo the damage of the past.

If you are not working with the original creditor, but with a collection agency, you can apply the same three questions:

1. *Are you willing to negotiate the amount of the debt?* The collection agency might be willing to reduce what you owe if you agree to promptly pay a reduced amount. They get some money in this way, even though it is less than the full amount. There is no certainty that the agency will go along with your offer, but it is worth a try.

2. *Are you willing to set up a payment plan?* Most collection agencies will agree to this, providing that you make all payments in a timely manner and that none of your checks bounce. If you miss a payment or bounce a check, the whole deal is going to be off the table; you won't get a second chance. As part of a negotiated payment plan, you should ensure that no added fees will go onto the balance, and that the entire debt will be discharged as soon as you have made all of the payments.

3. *Are you willing to permanently remove this item from my credit report?* You have to ensure that the collection agency will agree to this. Otherwise, you end up paying the debt but

the blemish remains. The offer to make a partial payment or to go onto a schedule of repayments is all well and good, but this is the only chance you have to leverage your offer. Make sure the collection agency agrees in writing to remove the negative item from your credit report as soon as you have kept your end of the bargain.

**911 SECRETS** You cannot expect negative items to be removed just because you pay them off.

Here is a sad but true story about how the right steps can still lead to the wrong outcome:

Steve and Gail called me to refinance their home loan. Their previous lender had stuck them in an 8.5 percent subprime loan with a two-year adjustment due, and they wanted to lower their rate and replace it with a fixed rate.

Because their credit score had fallen due to medical collections, they could not qualify for the refinance. Here's what had happened: Steve changed jobs and went to work for a new company. But his new boss missed a flight, which delayed his hire date by one week; naturally, this also delayed his medical coverage by one week. During the brief period when they did not have any medical insurance, Steve suffered a heart attack. The bills were enormous, as you would expect.

The bills went into past due status, so Steve and Gail had to scramble to pay them. They refinanced with a cash-out for part of it and emptied out their savings for the rest. They finally did pay off the bills, but had not negotiated in advance to get the past due status removed from their credit report. As a result, even though they were paid in full, the collections stayed on their credit report for *seven years*.

In this case, Steve and Gail—responsible, honest people whose credit scores and payment histories had been excellent before this incident—could not get a lower rate and had to live with the stigma of "past due" medical bills for the next seven years. They did the right thing but did not negotiate in advance to get the items removed. The right thing led to a very poor outcome.

Doing the right thing is not always enough. The harsh reality is that you have to also do the *smart* thing; always negotiate the removal of negative items in exchange for paying it off.

I had another couple call me to obtain a home loan. This couple had recently sold their home and forgot to notify one of their medical providers with the updated mailing address—an easy mistake to make in the chaos of the move. A $22 collection appeared, making it impossible for them to qualify for a new mortgage loan. Even though they acknowledged the error and promptly paid the outstanding balance, a negative delinquency remained for seven years and dropped their scores.

Here are three things they could have done to save themselves a lot of headache:

1. *Get a post office box or UPS mail drop.* A permanent address rather than a physical one enables you to continue getting mail if you move within the same town or city, without delay or disruption in the flow of your mail.
2. *File the change of address form with the post office, but also notify everyone yourself.* Be sure you provide a new address to *all* of your creditors, including anyone you have made payments to over the past two years and, of course, everyone to whom you currently owe money. In addition to your creditors, this includes doctors, dentists, newspaper and magazine subscriptions: creditors you

might not make regular payments to, but people who, nevertheless, want their money. File the forms with the post office, but make your own notification as well.

3. *Follow up with providers if you do not hear from them.* In case your notification gets lost, don't assume that silence means forgiveness. It's your responsibility to make sure that creditors can find you.

Don't fool yourself into believing that if "they can't find you they can't bill you." Outstanding bills *always* end up on your credit report, so make sure they know how to contact you at all times

## Dealing with Debt Settlement and Credit Repair Agencies

You may have some delinquencies and want to take steps to clean up your credit and raise your score. Paying off debts with negotiated settlements and repayment plans and, of course, agreements to remove negatives from the record are all part of the process. But is it smart to hire a company to help you repair your credit?

Two kinds of companies are quite visible in the whole "credit-fixing" industry. First is the *debt settlement* company. These organizations offer to negotiate your debt for you, often settling outstanding items for less than the amount owed. They advertise heavily, at times making promises they cannot always keep. A debt settlement company might be able to *reduce* your debts in some cases, but settled debts are still likely to stay on your credit report for seven years.

Pouring funds into these types of companies is likely to be a poor decision. Let's crunch some numbers. A customer contacts a debt settlement company to help with $30,000 in credit card debt. The company may get the creditors to settle for less, or they put the account in dispute. However, the agency's fee is 16 percent of the amount settled, *and* the customer gets a federal 1099 form at the end of the year for the difference—yes, the unpaid portion is taxable. So if the $30,000 debt is settled for $20,000, that leaves $10,000 of taxable income, or $2,800 in taxes due (if you're in a 28 percent tax bracket). Since the debt settlement agency also charged $3,200 (16 percent of the amount settled), the real net outcome of this was a saving of only:

- unpaid portion of $30,000 debt: $10,000
- less debt settlement agency fee: $3,200
- less taxes on $10,000 at 28 percent: $ 2,800
- net savings: $ 4,000

So you end up paying $20,000 to settle the debt and another $6,000 in taxes and fees. Debt settlement under these conditions is hardly a bargain There's a reason why these companies have been under fire and heavily scrutinized in recent years — they should be. Many of these companies take advantage of people at their most financially vulnerable times and disguise themselves as a solution. The second type of organization is referred to as *credit repair*. These companies charge a monthly fee or flat fee to dispute items on your credit report. Typically, a company like this runs through your credit report putting items in dispute so that when your credit is pulled, the derogatory items are not included in the scoring. This does raise your credit score, but only temporarily. Instead, consider using your money not on the costly fees of a credit repair company, but to pay down these debts and work towards a *permanent* solution. Lenders have caught onto the credit repair companies' tactics, and may no longer approve loan applicants with multiple disputed items on their credit report. This means that strategies centered on disputing items to temporarily raise your score in hopes to get a loan approved no longer work.

According to the attorney general of Texas, Greg Abbott, anything a credit repair agency can do, you can do yourself.*

---

* http://www.oag.state.tx.us/consumer/credit_repair.shtml.

You can dispute an item on your credit report without the help of an outside company. If you feel an item legitimately needs to be disputed, write a letter providing an explanation as to why you feel it needs to be removed. Be prepared to provide backup documentation if necessary. A sample letter follows (be sure to send the letter to *all* agencies reporting information in error):

---

To:
    Equifax
    P.O. Box 740241
    Atlanta GA 30374-0241
    (800) 392-7816
    www.equifax.com

    Experian
    P.O. Box 2104
    Allen TX 75013
    (888) 397-3742
    www.experian.com/reportaccess

    Trans Union
    P.O. Box 2000
    Chester, PA 19022
    (866) 887-2673
    www.transunion.com

RE: Social Security Number:_____

Dear Ladies or Gentlemen:

    I am writing to request immediate removal of the following erroneous information from my credit report. Please update my file and forward me a copy of my complete, fair, and accurate credit report.

    Please send me the names, business addresses, and telephone number for each individual you contact to verify these accounts and balances to enable me to follow-up with them regarding these accounts.

I am enclosing a copy of my latest credit report with the relevant accounts highlighted. I have also added notations for your reference.

Item #: 1
Creditor: _____
Date of delinquency: _____
Explanation: The delinquency is over seven years old. This item is old and obsolete under 15 U.S.C. § 1681c. Please remove it from my credit report.

Item # 2
Creditor:_____
Date of delinquency: _____
Explanation: The delinquency is over seven years old. This item is old and obsolete under 15 U.S.C. § 1681c. Please remove it from my credit report.

Sincerely,
Enclosures: List all items enclosed

As shocking as it might seem, I know for a fact that credit repair agencies are only successful about 10 percent of the time. I learned this from questioning my seminar attendees. The Bureau of Labor Statistics (www.bls.gov) estimates that from 2009 through

911 SECRETS

There is nothing a credit repair agency can do for a fee that you cannot do on your own. It's better to save the fee and put that money toward your debts.

2016, the credit repair and debt collection industry is going to grow as astounding as 23 percent, much faster than virtually any other industry. Most of that increase will come from debt collection services provided to medical providers and government agencies. An independent study concluded that debt collection is a thriving business as well. In 2005 alone, U.S. businesses sent a whopping $141 billion in delinquent consumer debt to collections; collection agencies collected $51 billion in past due debt, keeping approximately one-fourth of the total as profit.

Remember these action points:

1. *Doing nothing is not an option.* Taking no action and avoiding phone calls or throwing away brightly colored past due notices only makes it worse. As frightening as it is to face these problems, ignoring them does not make them disappear.

2. *Do not allow collection callers to use intimidation.* It is against the law for collectors to make threats or to call you repeatedly with harassing or threatening statements. Know your rights. To enforce those rights, document the harassment. First mail a "do not call" letter to the creditor and their collection agency. Include your name, account information, and instructions about how they can contact you. Send this letter with a return receipt to establish proof of the date you sent it. Next, keep a log of the date and time of every call. Include the name of the person making the call. Be aware of your legal rights. These include:

   - Collection calls can be made only at reasonable hours. This usually means between 8 A.M. and 9 P.M.
   - Collection calls cannot be made to you at work if you instruct them to phone you only at home. A favorite tactic is to embarrass you into paying the debt to avoid getting in trouble with your employer.
   - Download and read the Federal Trade Commission (FTC) ruling on the Fair Debt Collection Practices Act

(FDCPA), 806(5). Check the FTC web site at http://www
.ftc.gov/os/statutes/fdcpa/commentary.htm

You should also be aware of how the debt collection
business works. Statistics reveal that one company, Portfolio
Recovery Associates (PRA) purchased 658 debt portfolios
with face value of $16.4 billion over a 10-year period. Their
cost: only $415.4 million, or about two and a half cents on the
dollar. The company collected about seven and a half cents
on the dollar of debt, meaning they tripled their gross investment. In 2005, PRA reported net profits of $36.8 million. My
point: Debt collection is a profitable business because companies buy debt for a few pennies. So they have a lot of room
to negotiate with you and to settle debt for much less than
the original face value. (Cited at http://www.debtcollection-
answers.com/Debt-Collection-Statistics.html.)

## A Medical Emergency

After reviewing credit reports day after day, I began to notice a common thread: most reports included medical collections that were
negatively affecting their score. With each collection was a disheart-
ening story that caused my concern to grow and sparked a desire to
find a solution. I got involved. I submitted a bill to Congress. This
bill is the Medical Debt Relief Act of 2009.

Here is how this came about: In 2008, an elderly couple showed
up in my office in search of a reasonable mortgage. I discovered
at once that they could not qualify for the best rates due to a small
medical collection item on their credit report. It struck me as wrong
that an isolated incident like this could drag down someone's credit
score, and I was curious to find out how many people were affected
in the same way. What I found out was mind-blowing.

I was already aware that an outstanding medical collection
remains on your credit report for seven years like other debts,
*even if you repay the debt.* This is not fair, especially if your credit history has otherwise been pristine. In addition, medical billing is an

error-prone system run by third party billing agents. Americans don't ask to have heart attacks or accidents, so I asked the question— "Why is medical collection debt treated the same as other types of debt?" What I *realized* was that changing the law could boost the U.S. economy not by millions, but by *billions*—due to improved credit scoring rules for medical delinquencies. So I contacted U.S. House Representative Mary Jo Kilroy of Ohio's 15th Congressional District and began the long (and expensive) process of crafting a new piece of federal legislation. The result was HR 3421, the Medical Debt Relief Act of 2009. This bill amends the Fair Credit Reporting Act and was introduced in the U.S. House of Representatives on July 30, 2009. Under existing rules, even a medical debt of only a few dollars can drag down the scoring enough to disqualify home, auto, and other loan applicants or result in higher interest rates. Under the new bill, credit bureaus will be required to remove medical debts from credit reports within 30 days after debt repayment.

The idea gained steam as it moved through Congressional review. In addition to its original sponsor Representative Kilroy, its co-sponsors include the Chair of the House Committee on Financial Services Subcommittee on Financial Institutions and Consumer Credit, Representative Luis Gutierrez of the Illinois 4th Congressional District, as well as dozens of additional co-sponsor representatives.

The bill is a win-win-win. First, non–credit related debts will not impact credit scores, enabling consumers to get interest rates gauged by their *real* credit histories. Second, medical providers benefit because patients have an incentive to repay the debt improving their percentage of successful collections. And third, the government and the country benefits as the economy is stimulated by more purchasing power and the resulting tax revenues from hospital/physician income.

Does this new legislation affect you? It will, especially in light of the fact that millions of Americans are adversely affected under the past rules. A total of 72 million Americans suffer from this, and medical debt is the number one cause of bankruptcy.*

There is much more to the collections business than most Americans know, and knowledge is power. Collection agencies are not your friends; they have one single goal—to *collect your money*. So your ability to negotiate is key. I even recommend practicing with a friend or family member to role-play the scenario. I have found that being nice makes it easier to deal with a collector rather than being mean or abrupt. The more you understand how it all works, the better equipped you are to protect yourself. Expanding on this point, the next chapter explains how the U.S. credit system works.

---

* Sara R. Collins, Jennifer L. Kriss, Michelle M. Doty, and Sheila D. Rustgi, "Losing Ground: How the Loss of Adequate Health Insurance Is Burdening Working Families—Findings from the Commonwealth Fund Biennial Health Insurance Surveys, 2001–2007," *The Commonwealth Fund*, August 20, 2008.

# CHAPTER 6

# The Credit System and How It Works

It doesn't matter how good looking you are, what kind of car you drive, or how impressive your possessions. Your credit score doesn't take any of this into consideration. There's nothing sexy about credit, and looks are often deceiving. What *does* matter is what your score reveals—the conclusion that lenders, insurance companies, and employers draw about you is frequently based on inaccurate credit reports.

That's not the exception; it's the rule. A full 79 percent of all credit reports contain at least one error.* This error rate is staggering. Imagine what you would think upon finding out that doctors misdiagnosed patients 8 out of 10 times. Or what if an NFL quarterback threw an interception on 8 out of every 10 passes? As Donald Trump would say, "You're fired!" So why is it acceptable for 79 percent of all American credit reports to have at least one error? You see, the American credit system is broken and full of errors. But we all have to work within the system, or the system will beat us.

Over half (54 percent) have wrong demographics such as misspelled names, outdated addresses, or mistakes in identity; 22 percent

---

* "Mistakes Do Happen: A Look at Errors in Consumer Credit Reports," U.S. Public Interest Research Group (U.S. PIRG), www.uspirg.org/home/reports/report-archives/financial-privacy–security/financial-privacy–security/mistakes-do-happen-a-look-at-errors-in-consumer-credit-reports, June 17, 2004.

listed a mortgage twice or included a mortgage and balance that had been refinanced and eliminated. And 30 percent showed open balances on accounts that had been closed.

Here's an example of how errors affect you. William was the third person in his family with the same name as his father and grandfather. He was receiving notice after notice from credit card companies, advising that his interest rate was being raised. Three accounts changed in a short period of time, from 2.9 percent to 27.9 percent, from 5.9 percent to 32.9 percent, and from 7.9 percent to 34.9 percent. That's not all. J.P. Morgan–Chase raised his minimum payment from 2 percent to 5 percent. Why was this happening? When William was attending school at Oklahoma University for his bachelor's degree, he had received a lot of credit card offers and he signed up for all of them. He had been disciplined and never used his accounts. The companies kept raising his limit over five years, over and over. In fact, Citibank had been so generous that they had raised his original line from $1,000 to $30,000.

Lacking financial assistance from his parents due to the economic downturn, and due to the loss of his father's business, William felt his only choice was to charge his tuition and living expenses on his credit cards once he moved on to law school at Georgetown. This was the first time he had ever gone into debt on his credit card accounts. He also knew he would be able to pay down and off his credit cards once he got out of school and into the practice of law. What William didn't expect was that his interest rates would spiral out of control. Not only did his rates climb drastically, his credit card companies also reduced his lines of credit.

He was so close to his final goal of being a lawyer and was set to graduate in six months, but his financial life was in jeopardy. Why was everything out of control? William finally picked up the phone and called one of the companies and he couldn't believe what he heard. They said he had made late payments and the pending bankruptcy was hurting him. He asked, "What late payments and what bankruptcy?" He pulled his credit report only to discover that his father— who had the same name—had filed bankruptcy, and his information had ended up on William's credit report. His father's financial struggles now transferred to William, and the damage was already done.

The error on William's credit report was big. Errors can be very minor with the same outcome. Brett and Heather walked into my office one day to apply for a mortgage loan. They were well dressed, well educated, and articulate. They had good jobs, substantial income, and were able to offer a large down payment. At first glance, they were the perfect applicants. Checking their credit reports seemed like a formality, but it turned out to be a disaster. They were devastated to learn that their loan would be denied due to their current scores. Although they had been responsible with their credit, they, like many other Americans, had three medical collections totaling a mere $250 that had taken a huge toll on their credit scores. They had proof that the negative items were to be removed from their credit report by agreement but in spite of the agreement, the action hadn't been taken as promised, and Brett had not followed up on it. The biggest problem was that the seller of the house wanted to close in 10 days and even had back-up offers. This didn't give Brett and Heather time to get the problem fixed, so they ended up losing out on their dream home altogether.

This story is not unique. Whether it's medical collections, cosigned debt, or some unforeseen situation (job loss, divorce, bankruptcy, or any of life's hurdles), this can happen to anyone and often *does*.

## The Meaning of Your Score

You might not realize this, but you don't have a single score. Everyone has three scores within FICO (the best-known system, developed in 1958 by the Fair Isaac Corporation). These are the scores calculated by the three credit-reporting bureaus, and they are going to be different because they do not all receive identical information about your credit or inquiries about you. For example, let's say your Experian score is 650, TransUnion is 723, and Equifax is 799. A lender will not average these. They will throw out the top and bottom scores and use the middle one.

Always think of your credit score as your financial DNA. As far as lenders are concerned, that three-digit number is all they need to know about you.

This difference in scoring is important not only when it comes to getting a loan approved at a good rate; it can also affect your insurance rates and your ability to get a job. Many employers obtain copies of applicants' credit reports as part of the interview process. Because credit scores are indicators of financial responsibility, the selection of one person over another for a job could come down to the difference of a few points on a credit report. Under the Fair Credit Reporting Act, you are not required to grant permission to a prospective employer to pull your credit report. Refusing, however, could be viewed as "taking the Fifth," and while employers will not admit it, your refusal may affect their final decision. So before applying for jobs, it makes sense to get copies of all three reports and make sure that there are no errors on any of them.

Why is this necessary? Many assumptions are in force regarding credit scoring and how those scores are calculated. These wrong assumptions, or a series of myths, include:

**Myth #1:** *Lenders must report accurate information.* A broad assumption among consumers is that lenders *must* report information correctly. If you believe this, think again. Of course lenders are expected to provide correct information. But just as a fast-food employee might forget to include your fries, mistakes are common. Ultimately it is your responsibility to make sure your credit information is accurate, and that any mistakes are removed.

**Myth #2:** *Paying off credit cards every month will give me a higher credit score.* It's amazing that if you use your debit card at the store the money disappears from your checking account right away. But if you pay off your credit card in full every month your score will not be affected for up to 30 days. For example, let's say you travel for work 20 days out of the month and you charge all of your business trips on your credit card. If you have a line of credit for $50,000 and you use $45,000, you are at 90 percent capacity. Then your company reimburses you the entire $45,000, and you pay off the credit card. Your credit score should go up immediately, right? Wrong. The credit card company only reports to the credit bureaus once per month. For example, let's say on September 15 your Citibank card balance is $45,000 and on September 20 you pay off the card. If Citibank reports for the month on September 15, then your credit score on September 15 is based on a $45,000 balance. This keeps your credit score low for the next 30 days, until Citibank reports again, on October 15.

**Myth #3:** *Paying off a credit card with a high balance will have larger effect on my credit score.* Under the FICO scoring system, a credit card with a $20,000 balance on a $25,000 limit is scored exactly the same as a $200 balance on a card with a $250 limit. Both of them are at 80 percent capacity. So paying off the higher balance will have the exact same impact as paying off the $200 balance. Of course, the $20,000 card will cost you more interest; but if your goal is to improve your credit score, pay off the cards with smaller balances first.

**Myth #4:** *I have a high income, so I should have a high credit score.* Credit scoring does not take into account how much money you make. As a matter of fact, that information is not provided to the credit bureaus at all.

**Myth #5:** *There is an effective means to predict who will become delinquent or default on a loan.* The truth is, FICO tracking has become less efficient in recently years. One study concluded that in 2001 there was a 31-point spread between defaulted borrowers and those who pay on time. By 2006, the spread had fallen to only 10 points.*

In practice, the credit-scoring industry is a game played by lenders, borrowers, and the agencies themselves. This does not mean the system lacks value, however, there are steps you as a consumer can take to maximize your credit score. You have to know how the score is calculated and play by the rules of the game.

911 SECRETS

Credit scoring is a game that lenders and agencies play. If you are going to win, you better know how the game is played.

## The Credit Scoring Game

The methods used to calculate your creditworthiness are complex, mysterious, and may even seem illogical to most people. The confusion comes from the fact that several different and conflicting methods are used, and seemingly innocent decisions can have a big negative impact on your credit score.

Your score—the bottom line used to decide whether to grant credit and if so at what rate—is affected by many different factors, most of which are within your control. If you want to raise a low credit score, you can take steps today to begin the process. Hiring a company to magically improve your credit can be expensive and is not necessary. As a matter of fact, it can do more harm than good.

Credit score confusion arises from the fact that there are many methods used to define "good" or "bad" credit. A perfect score is 850 and the lowest possible score is 300 under FICO. The purpose

---

\* Dean Foust and Aaron Pressman, "Credit Scores: Not-So-Magic Numbers," *BusinessWeek*, February 7, 2008.

of credit scoring is to distinguish the degree of likelihood that any one person will repay debt in a timely manner or if he or she is likely to default. It measures a lender's risk.

The analysis of credit is based on credit data reported by three credit agencies: TransUnion, Equifax, and Experian. Before a lender will grant credit, a credit report is requested from one or more of these three, and that report is the primary basis for a lender's decision. These decisions include whether or not to approve a loan application, the interest rate assessed, and levels of collateral required to secure the loan (percentage of down payment required for a mortgage loan, for example). The very first problem you face when lenders look at your credit score is that the three agencies will not necessarily have identical information. If you dispute an erroneous item with one agency and have it removed, that does not mean it is also removed from the two other agencies. They operate independently.

## Scoring Methods

The methods used to develop your credit score are not isolated; your credit history is compared to other consumers as part of the rating. For example, if you have two late payments beyond 30 days on your record, your rating is determined based on statistical risks of other people with the same history. So if having two late payments equals a strong chance of default, the situation lowers your score.

Under the Federal Reserve Board's Regulation B (which put the Equal Credit Opportunity Act into effect), scoring cannot be made based on race, religion, sex, or marital status. The rules also require that rating systems have to be statistically sound and, in the event the credit is denied, a lender has to disclose the specific reason. Having a score that is too low is not adequate; lenders have to explain exactly why credit was denied. For example, lenders have to peg excessive delinquencies, too many outstanding balances, or too many high-balance accounts outstanding as their reason for denying credit or curtailing terms of an existing credit account.

Since there are several systems in wide use, your score is likely to be unclear, especially if the three agencies produce different scoring numbers. The FICO scoring is widely used, so non-FICO methods are likely to mimic the FICO scores. Because they are not the same, these non-FICO scoring methods often are called FAKO. Some lenders rely on scoring systems sold by the rating agencies that cost less than FICO and mimic FICO scoring, often creating wide disparity among ratings.

Under FICO, your score is going to be based on five criteria. Each makes up a specific percentage of your overall score. This breakdown is shown below.

These criteria are:

*Payment history:* This accounts for 35 percent of your score. All history of payment, including late payments, is taken into account on mortgages, credit card, auto loans, and revolving accounts. Since this constitutes the highest percentage of your score, avoiding any late payments does more than anything else to keep your credit score high.

*Credit capacity:* This is 30 percent of your FICO score. It consists of the ratio between revolving credit debt and total credit limits. When you pay off a debt you lower your utilization, improving your score. However, if you close a revolving credit account, it actually reduces your overall score by lowering the basis for calculating the ratio. A problem with utilization: If you are carrying debt equal to 90 percent of a $1,000 line of credit, that is a 90 percent utilization ratio, even though the credit limit is low. It is counted the same way as carrying $9,000 on a $10,000 credit limit. The second part of capacity is a comparison between the number of cards with balances, versus the total cards you have. For example, if you have 10 credit card accounts and only three have balances, your capacity is 30 percent. If you close five of those accounts not being used, you end up with three out of five cards with balances. That is 60 percent capacity. This hurts your credit score. The goal of capacity is to always be under 50 percent.

*Length of credit history:* 15 percent of your total score is tied to how long you've been using credit. So the longer you have had credit, especially if you have been making timely payments, the higher your credit history score is likely to be. In today's lending environment, lenders are looking for you to have at least three established accounts with a *minimum* of a 12-month history.

*Type of credit:* 10 percent of your score is made up of the types of credit used: installment payments, revolving credit accounts, credit cards, or consumer finance, for example. Consumer finance is considered higher risk than the other types, so avoiding high-risk forms of credit improves your score. This is granted by companies specializing in underwriting financing for any organization that does not directly offer credit cards. For example, Lens Crafters lets you buy glasses on credit, but the Lens Crafters bill comes from GE Credit.

*Recent credit inquiries:* The final 10 percent is made up of the number of credit inquiries appearing on your credit report. Recent searches and the amount of credit recently granted go into this number. When multiple credit inquiries are made in a short period of time, it can hurt your score. So if you apply for new credit cards or allow an auto dealer to pull your report, it can have a negative impact. Activity like this is considered risky because a rapid accumulation of new debt could take place soon after inquiries take place. Every potential lender knows this, and as a result, your score falls when a lot of inquiries are made in recent weeks or months.

911 SECRETS    Knowing the elements that go into your credit score will allow you to control it before it controls you.

## Your Credit Report

Your credit *score* is the ratings number assigned to you as a result of your credit history and current credit activity. Your credit *report* shows the itemized details used to arrive at the score. Each of the three reporting agencies develops your report based on information they receive, and they do not always have identical outcomes. Basically, though, your credit report includes:

- A summary of negative issues (bankruptcy, liens or judgments, delinquent accounts, and late payments)
- A listing of credit card accounts including issuer, account numbers, credit limit, current balance, and payment history—as well as a distinction between on-time payments and those falling into the negative category
- Mortgages and other debts including original loan amount, current balance, monthly payment, and number of late payments if any
- Credit inquiries
- Credit capacity

All of this information goes into the calculation of your credit score. Remember, there are three agencies, so you are going to have three different credit scores. The three might also have errors in items as straightforward as your personal information: current and past addresses, aliases, and marital status, for example.

It's your responsibility to correct errors on your credit report. Don't assume someone else will fix them for you.

## Situations I Have Seen First-Hand

Now that you have the nuts and bolts, a broad overview of the credit system and how it works, you should ask, "Why is it important for me to check my credit reports and make sure they are accurate?" Another important question is: "How can I improve my credit score?" Remember, two items—payment history and credit capacity—make up 65 percent of your overall score. So any steps you can take now will gradually improve your credit score.

The credit score has a significant impact on your life. To demonstrate, following are some situations I have seen firsthand.

### *The Convenient Subscription Deal*

Mark used an automatic bill pay feature on a credit card for the newspaper subscription on a credit card he almost never used. He was an honest guy who paid his bills on time, worked hard, and followed the rules. But he neglected to open the monthly statement because it usually showed a zero balance; he forgot that he had placed his subscription on that card. The subscription charge was on there, though, and it went past due and into collection. His credit score dropped to 560 as a result of his not opening the statement and making a timely payment. This was a costly mistake. It took years to recover from a small oversight, but this was entirely his responsibility.

### *The Inquiry Effect*

Bob and Sandra were prequalified to build their dream home. As the house was built, they shopped for furniture, appliances, and other items to fill their home. They were excited that their American dream was about to be realized after years of careful financial management. At last their hard work was going to pay off. But trouble began when we reviewed their updated credit reports. I had advised Bob during our initial meeting how important it was *not* to purchase any items during the loan process. Sandra had

123

not been present at the meeting because she had to work, and Bob never shared the information with her. He didn't want to disappoint her by telling her she couldn't shop. Their scores were unexpectedly low as a result of the inquiries they had authorized. Their American dream turned into a nightmare when I had to tell them they could not qualify for the loan. They had to wait until the inquiries fell off of the report several months later. They found out too late how the system works. Meanwhile, property values went up, and they were forced to settle for a smaller house for the same money—all because of excessive *inquiries* on their credit reports. This is why people need to understand and pay attention to the credit system and how it works.

911 SECRETS    Never make large purchases or open new accounts when a lender is evaluating your loan application.

How is your credit? Are you at risk for one of these unexpected surprises based on errors in your credit report or inadvertent negative items resulting from innocent behavior? The only way to know is to review your credit report at least once per year. Amazingly, 144 million worked-age adult Americans—that's 64 percent—have not reviewed their credit report during the past year.*

It is unlikely that many people can avoid being a part of this system. In 2000, there were 159 million credit cardholders in the United States, 173 million by 2006, and an estimated 181 million by 2010. At the close of 2009, there were 576.4 million credit cards in circulation, averaging 3.5 cards per cardholder.[†]

---

* National Foundation for Credit Counseling, 2009 Financial Literacy Survey, April 2009.

† "Credit card statistics, industry facts, debt statistics," Ben Woolsey and Matt Schulz, http://www.creditcards.com/credit-card-news/credit-card-industry-facts-personal-debt-statistics-1276.php, May 13, 2010.

Having a lot of credit cards isn't a problem as long as payments are made on time, right? Well, more than one in four—26 percent or 58 million people—say they do *not* pay their credit card bills on time. This not only reduces their credit scores, but creates an incredible profit center for card issuers in the form of late fees.*

## Strategies for Taking Control

To take control of your credit and avoid becoming one of those statistics—and to increase your credit score—follow these steps:

1. *Pull your credit report today.* Make sure it is based on the FICO scoring to make comparisons valid, and pull reports at least once per year, and more frequently if you have gone through major credit-changing events such as divorce, bankruptcy, or foreclosure.
2. *Pay off revolving debt before applying for financing.* If you pay off your existing revolving debt, especially on accounts with finance companies, you will raise your score. Pay the accounts down to a zero balance 45 to 60 days before applying for new financing to maximize your score. And remember, don't use those accounts in the meantime.
3. *Shop for financing before signing a contract.* Always get preapproved before ever signing on the bottom line. Many lenders make a lot of money charging high interest rates to customers who have fallen in love with a new car, home, or product and will blindly go along with the financing arranged by the inhouse finance company. By getting preapproval you can focus on negotiating a better price rather than on financing your purchase. Don't shop based on "payment" but on the true overall cost. Remember, many companies send out credit applications to multiple lenders and take the fastest approval, not the best terms. It's fast for them and bad for you.

---

* National Foundation for Credit Counseling, 2009 Financial Literacy Survey, April 2009.

4. *Pay for a credit monitoring system—this is valuable credit insurance.* A credit monitoring program costs about $100 per year, but protects you from potential credit issues. You are immediately notified when inquiries are made or when delinquencies are reported. This allows you to *prevent* errors and other problems in advance (including identity theft), rather than trying to fix them after they have appeared on your report.

5. *Avoid negative scoring due to excessive inquiries.* There are two types of inquiries: *hard pulls* and *soft pulls*. A soft pull is any inquiry that does not affect your score, such as inquiries by your insurance company and requests you make for your own credit report. A hard pull can affect your credit adversely and remains on the credit report for as long as one year. This is generated whenever you give someone else permission to get a copy of your credit report. This could be a perspective landlord or a potential lender. Applying for a credit card is a common form of hard pull. Every hard pull lowers your score. The inquiry also shows up on your report and will be visible to anyone reviewing it. Multiple inquiries can create great damage. So if you are building a new home and you open accounts (or put in applications) for three credit cards, and three other stores (home improvement, flooring, window treatments), that's a total of up to six hard pulls and can have a negative effect on your credit score.

**911 SECRETS**  A small investment in credit monitoring is a must and can prevent huge problems later.

There are many secrets and strategies to managing your credit score. Knowledge and diligence are key. You need to know how your innocent actions can result in damaging your score, and having negative items may show up on your report as a result. You can manage your score by keeping inquiries down and by managing capacity ratios *before* you apply for credit anywhere. This will result in better approvals and lower interest rates. Basically, joining a minority of people who are even aware of how their credit score is calculated makes you a better-informed consumer and a smarter credit user.

The problems you can face as a result of your credit score can appear in just about any situation, even those where you don't directly use credit (such as in job applications). For most Americans, the event of greatest importance and consequence is in financing a home. This is likely the largest purchase you will ever make, and yet many people do little or no research when selecting a Realtor, understanding the cost of homes in the area, or financing options. Some spend more time researching refrigerator brands than they do when they buy a home. The next chapter explores this topic and provides you with valuable guidelines for being a smart homebuyer.

# CHAPTER 7

# Buying Real Estate Is Not a Joke

Do you need to qualify your expert? You have heard the old adage, "If it sounds too good to be true, it probably is." Many a parent has drilled this into the heads of their children in the hopes that it would repeat in their heads forever as they moved into adulthood. I've used it myself when consulting with potential homebuyers about financing options. In order to illustrate how incredibly important it is to interview and qualify your lender, realtor, or builder, I want to tell you a story about a terrible injustice that occurred right near my own hometown of Dallas, Texas.

A well-known semi-custom builder began constructing very nice homes in the area—nice enough to attract a wide array of potential homeowners from all different backgrounds. The majority of these people were not financial experts, and many had not obtained prequalification from a lender beforehand. When visiting the model home, they were greeted by friendly sales people and the smell of fresh-baked cookies. They were encouraged to walk through the beautifully decorated model, admiring the custom paint colors, floor-to-ceiling windows, and enough bedrooms and bathrooms to accommodate a large family. It felt like a dream to these families, most of which had never imagined owning such a luxurious home.

After the tour, the head of the family was encouraged to spend a few minutes talking with the salesperson about the possibility of owning a new home in this subdivision. After all, didn't their family "deserve" to own this home? The seed of entitlement was planted, and suddenly it didn't seem so far-fetched. Eventually, they had to face the elephant in the room. This two-income family worked very hard, and had good jobs, but there was no way they made enough money to afford "all of this." The salesperson then brought out a flier with examples of monthly payments for their homes. Surely, this would offer the answers they needed to make an informed decision. There it was, the 3,500-square-foot model home they were standing in, costing $360,000, but with a monthly payment of only $1,540 a month. At that moment the family had begun to trust the expert, and was convinced that this builder and this home were the answer to their prayers.

Needless to say, these clients didn't have $360,000 cash, so of course they would need financing. This was not a problem, considering the fact that there was a loan officer sitting at a card table with a laptop, ready to prequalify them right then and there. Again, the emotions ran high (the kids were running around upstairs to call dibs on their new rooms), and they needed to get the contract written quickly, as the salesperson had already told them they were running out of lots that would accommodate such a large house. The loan officer pulled their credit and completed a loan application. They were provided information on a program that required no down payment, and could give them "flexible" payment options. It was even called an "option arm." Their payment coupons would give them different payment options, but they were only "required" to pay the $1,540 that they were comfortable paying. The happy homeowners closed on their new home a couple of months later, and lived happily ever after—almost.

Here's the truth.

1. The Option Adjustable-Rate Mortgage (ARM) payment these customers chose was a "negative amortization" payment.

The monthly payment wasn't even sufficient to cover the interest, meaning that every month, their balance *increased*.

2. The property taxes were not escrowed into the monthly payment, meaning that at the end of the year, these homeowners would receive a property tax bill for $8,500. The salesperson "sold" them on unimproved taxes, which are calculated on the dirt only; the tax assessor's office updates the taxes to show the true value after the house has been built. By that time the agent's commission check was cashed and the loan officer had provided them a disclosure somewhere in the mass of paperwork that advised them of the tax liability, although he had made a point not to spend too much time discussing it.

3. The interest rate on the Option ARM adjusted every six months after they moved into their home. The payment was $1,540 for six months, but quickly went to $1,700, $1,920, $2,100 — you get the point.

4. They would try to sell the home; however, there was also a prepayment penalty clause, meaning they would be penalized (six months of interest) for selling before the 36-month anniversary. They didn't have the equity in the home or the money to pay it out of pocket.

5. The worst part of all? The same program was sold to every other family in the subdivision. Within 18 months, 70 percent of the homes in the neighborhood were foreclosed, and those remaining in their homes watched their property values plummet as a result. They couldn't sell their homes because they all owed more than they were worth, and the once beautiful neighborhood became a ghost town.

The families were devastated, the developer didn't care, and the loan officer had folded up her card table and disappeared with a huge stack of cash and no legal liability for what she had done. To make matters worse, many of the families didn't qualify for the loans, and the loan officer used stated income loans to force them into loan contracts they couldn't possibly repay. This is what can happen when you trust the wrong people. You *must* do your homework when choosing a lender. Know the ins and outs of the loan program you choose, use a trusted and reputable lender, and remember what your parents told you: *If it sounds too good to be true, it probably is.*

One of the most shocking realities of American life is the way that some people buy and finance their homes. When they buy household appliances, 92 percent compare prices, but only 42 percent do the same when they buy and finance real estate.

## The Match Game: Getting *You* the Best Loan

If you fall for the hype some lenders put out, including the special no–down payment deals, teaser rates (initial low rates that balloon later), and other forms of creative financing, it is going to cost you. The "no closing costs" deals almost always include special "fees" offsetting your alleged savings, which are financed in with your purchase. There are always costs associated with a mortgage, and if you're not paying them, ask *who is?*

Many lenders have created quick interest ads with catchy phrases to get you in the door. They seduce you up front, and only later you find out that it is too good to be true. Buying a house is one of the biggest investments people will ever make, and yet every day customers walk into my office having done absolutely no homework, not even knowing what questions to ask and what answers they should be receiving. So many people do not take the time out of their day to meet with their lender in person, choosing instead to conduct business online. You *should always* attempt to sit down face-to-face with your lender or at least have a thorough phone conversation so you can discover if and why the lender is a good fit for you. All too often, people email or fax their information and never take the time to find out about the lender or the programs, more importantly, why a certain program is the right one for them.

Buying a home is one of the largest investments of your life. Take it seriously. Always know your loan and know your lender.

The only two questions many people care to ask are, "What is your interest rate?" and "Can you email or fax me a Good Faith Estimate?" This opens the door for lenders to bait-and-switch and gives you no guarantees, which can set you up for a *huge* surprise at the closing table. You must protect yourself at all times. Below, I have provided a list of 10 questions you must ask your lender to avoid becoming a statistic, like millions of Americans already have.

1. *How long have you been doing Federal Housing Administration/ Veterans Administration (FHA/VA) and conventional mortgages?* The answer you want to hear is that the lender is well-rounded and has many years experience in all of the major programs. This prevents a lender from placing you into a cookie-cutter, "one size fits all" loan that is not always the best option for you.

2. *What are all the loan products available to me?* Many loan officers only sell best commission products to you, and they have no conscience. It's all about profit. So make sure the lender has a range of choices and will work with you to compare the features, benefits, and costs of each one. If you are being rushed or steered into only one product, work with someone else unless they can show you why it's the only option available for you. How does a lender match you up with a loan he or she is encouraging you to buy? What are the criteria? Only by getting these questions answered can you make valid comparisons between products. Incidentally, if the lender is unable or unwilling to explain this to you, it means you need to find someone else to help you.

3. *What percentage of loans do you close on time?* This question may surprise many lenders because it is rarely asked, but a low percentage can mean expensive delays and even losing a deal. Closing dates are written into the real estate contract, and you do not want to risk losing a good loan or your future home because your lender is disorganized or lazy.

4. *Can you guarantee that your Good Faith Estimate is accurate and within $200?* The federal law requires lenders to supply you with a written summary of costs and fees you are required to pay to get financing and close the loan. The law is called the Real Estate Settlement Procedures Act (RESPA), and it is designed to prevent overcharging by lenders. The old bait and switch involves telling you one set of numbers and then, just before closing, replacing those with a new summary (including higher interest and points, and loan processing fees, for example) thousands of dollars higher. At this point, many buyers are trapped because they want to close on time. The law requires this to be given to you in writing. Fortunately, new legislation went into effect in January 2010 that aims to prevent this tactic, but buyers still must be on guard. A lender or broker can still present preliminary numbers in one format and then confuse the numbers later with the accurate one. A loan cannot be closed until seven business days *after* the Good Faith Estimate Truth in Lending disclosure is given to you. And the final annual percentage rate you end up being charged cannot be higher than 0.125 percent of the early Truth in Lending disclosure you were given. If rates have risen above this level, a lender must give you a redisclosure report before they can take you through the process and wait three days before closing the loan. The purpose of these changes is to prevent a lender from rushing you and, more importantly, from doing a bait-and-switch at the last minute.

Always call a time out when a lender is changing terms and conditions late in the game. Don't be a victim of a bait and switch.

5. *When can I refinance my loan? When can I not refinance my loan?* The terms of a loan include explanation of how and when it can be replaced. You may be subject to penalties if you try to refinance the existing loan too soon, and you need to know this before you sign. The best loan program places no limits or fees on refinancing, giving you the complete freedom to shop and obtain better rates and terms whenever they may be available.

6. *Are there prepayment penalties if the loan is paid off early?* This important distinction has to be studied with care. Some loans—the better ones—do not charge any penalties for accelerating your mortgage. Others limit the percentage of debt you can pay off without penalty each year. The fees can be quite high. The only reason for charging prepayment penalties is to guarantee the lender will collect interest (income) for a predetermined number of months. But as a consumer, why do you want to be locked in? Imagine how you would react to finding out that your credit card company allows you to only make the minimum monthly payment? You would shun that company and look for others that have no restriction. The same rule should be applied to your mortgage loan.

7. *Is this loan assumable?* The average first-time home buyer stays in that home for about five years; so when you apply for financing, remember that statistics say you are likely to be selling in a few years. In some cases, you want to be able to allow the new buyer to assume your current loan at your rate and remaining term (subject, of course, to approval by

the lender of the new buyer's creditworthiness). It's a great selling point when interest rates have gone up and you are sitting at a rate well below the current market, *if* the loan is assumable.

8. *Is my interest rate locked? Can you send me the rate lock agreement in writing?* A reputable lender will be willing to lock in an attractive rate *today* for a specified time frame, assuming your property has been identified. Some locked-in rates have a float-down option; your rate will never go higher, but if rates go down, you get a more attractive, lower rate within a certain time period.

**911 SECRETS** Never base a decision on a Good Faith Estimate alone.

9. *How long will it take me to break even if I pay points?* The break-even calculation is not difficult. A loan can be fixed at a lower rate as a result of additional points paid up front (discount points). This means you pay a slightly lower interest rate, but you are assessed points. Each "point" is equal to 1 percent of the amount being borrowed. The lender should be able to help you calculate this. For example, assume you are offered a $200,000 loan at 5.5 percent, but the rate can be lowered to 5.25 percent for one point. This point cost you $2,000 ($200,000 × 1 percent × 1 point). The difference in your monthly payment is going to be $31.17 per month ($1,135.58 for a 5.5 percent loan, versus $1,073.64 for a 5.0 percent loan). So if you save $31.17 per month, but the lower rate costs you $1,104.41, you will break even in about 60 months ($2,000 ÷ $31.17). That's just over five

years; statistically, you will only be in this home for about five years, therefore the reduced rate and points wouldn't make sense.

10. *Is my credit score affecting my interest rate?* The right answer, of course, is "yes." Rates will almost always be based on your FICO score. The best rates (usually what a lender advertises) are going to be available only for those with excellent scores. If your score is less than excellent, you may have to pay a higher rate for the same loan. Knowing this, take steps ahead of time to improve your score.

If you follow these 10 guidelines, you will avoid a lot of grief and save a lot of time and money. Throughout the housing and credit crisis that started in 2007 and 2008, people pointed fingers at lenders, deservedly so. In my opinion, what some of these unscrupulous predators did was tantamount to robbery, burglary, and probably felt like assault and battery. But many escaped prosecution, and they're still on the loose. Don't let your guard down or fall into the trap of thinking that the disreputable lenders of the past are simply gone. They have just changed their company names and moved, but they are still out there.

## The World of Real Estate Agents

Just like lenders, real estate agents make money on a commission basis. This means they are salespeople. Some agents think that lenders work for them and that their primary focus should be to help them get the sale. I will never forget the day that Lorraine's agent called to inform me that she had found her the "perfect house." Lorraine's agent also instructed me to "talk her into buying the house and closing very quickly," in order for her to have her paycheck in time to make her mortgage payment. I could not believe my ears. Was this really happening? I said to her agent, "I can't talk her into buying this or any house." She got angry and said, "I am going to send her to a mortgage person that will follow my instructions."

Just as you need to find a lender with integrity, you need to apply the same standard to a real estate agent. The way most people hire an agent is often the least recommended. You are likely to be a cold call into a real estate office or open house. The agent sitting in the office is likely to be there instead of out making sales because he or she is the newest member of the firm. This means they may be also the least experienced, put there because (a) none of the more productive agents want to lose time selling and (b) the broker knows that the "agent of the day" stuck in the office might pick up a few clients just by being there. Although many successful agents are present at open houses, primary agents may also talk a novice into house-sitting for them. The deal they make is that if they get a buyer from the open house, the primary agent will split his or her fee with the novice. This is often an opportunity to give out business cards and bait serious buyers to show them other homes in addition to the open house, but there is no guarantee that the agent on site is experienced.

Never confuse "showing up" with experience. A novice agent often is assigned the highest visibility, meaning *you* are not always meeting the most experienced agent in that company.

As a group, real estate salespeople are often overlooked in the critical evaluation of how homes are bought and sold. Through all the mortgage mess, some real estate professionals have gotten off scot free, even though they have done some of the most dastardly thing to home buyers. It is always a case of *caveat emptor*, or, buyer beware.

There is a litmus test you need to give real estate agents before you decide to trust them with your transaction and your money. To simplify what can be a very daunting process, I've organized this test into three parts: questions that will help you decide which realtor to hire, questions to ask your realtor once you've narrowed in on your desired neighborhood, and the questions to ask your realtor when you've found the house you wish to purchase. Before deciding upon which realtor to work with, these three questions will help you decide who the best fit is for you:

1. *How much time a week do you devote to real estate, or is real estate your part-time job?* If this is a part-time job you should reconsider working with the agent. Considering how much money you are going to spend on finding a home, you need (and deserve) a full-time, qualified professional. Believe it or not, many, and I mean many, are in the business for the weekends as a way to make ends meet. Ask them how many times it took them to pass the real estate exam. You want to work with an agent who knows what he or she is doing in any transaction, and getting credentials should not be an afterthought. The real estate exam is not too tough for most reasonably intelligent people to pass with some basic study, on the first try. You'll see why the difference between a weekend salesperson and a full-time professional is important as you read the following questions.

2. *When are you not available? Are our schedules compatible?* If the agent spends days on another job (their "real" job?), that is a clue that you should move on to someone else. Real estate is all about timing, and if you can't get a contract delivered within a narrow time limit, that makes a lot of difference. Not being able to reach your agent after hours or on weekends could cost you the perfect home you're trying to buy.

3. *Have you ever personally bought or sold a home?* Let's be real about this. There is something about real-time experience that is hard to beat. You should expect your real estate professional to have owned real estate in the past. For example, would you hire a stockbroker who had never put money into the market? Probably not. The same should apply to hiring a real estate salesperson.

Later on in the process, ask your realtor the following three questions to ensure the neighborhood you have found is a good long-term investment:

4. *How many foreclosures are in the neighborhood?* This is a key question. Your agent should know exactly how many homes are in foreclosure; the truth is, every realtor should have this information at his or her fingertips and be willing to share it with you. While someone may have gotten an exciting "steal" by purchasing a house valued at $230,000 for only $200,000, your future neighbors may have purchased theirs for only $180,000, and the people across the street got a deal for only $160,000! This information is of great importance because it can be an indicator that market values may continue to fall in the area.

5. *How many houses are owned by investors?* There is an important distinction between properties that are owner-occupied and those held for investment. Just like the foreclosure question, a professional real estate agent should have this information already and be willing and able to share it with you. A larger percentage of owner-occupied homes is desirable because owners are more likely than tenants to keep their property well maintained, report crimes like drug dealing and burglary, and care about neighborhood conditions. Tenants are not invested in terms of equity or place, and are probably thinking ahead to move somewhere else to buy a home—if they think that far ahead. If a neighborhood has a high percentage of tenants, then the investment value of homes is not going to be as strong as elsewhere.

**911 SECRETS**
A neighborhood filled with investment properties is not generally going to hold value as well as a more established neighborhood with a majority of owner-occupied homes.

6. *How well do you know school districts, builders and obstacles in this area?* A qualified agent should be extremely well versed in these matters because they determine value and desirability of living there. What about traffic flow, congestion, and noise? Have any lawsuits been filed suing builders for construction-related problems? Are there any known pollution problems or nuisances you need to know? You can certainly research these matters for yourself by reading headlines for the local paper over the past year; but your agent should help you find these answers rather than "forgetting" to mention them. Ultimately, the value of your property and your quality of life are going to be directly affected by these issues. So you have to find out *before* you buy, and not after, that the bargain-priced home you're looking at sits at the end of a major airport.

Once you've found the house you've been searching for, make sure to ask these three final questions to ensure you have diligently researched every aspect of the home-buying process:

7. *How much are the utility bills for the house?* As a hard-and-fast rule, always insist on seeing a full year's utility bills for any house you're thinking seriously of making an offer on. What you see might change your mind. If you're moving from a moderate climate like the West Coast to the Deep South, you don't want to be surprised. You may learn that air conditioning and heating are going to cost you $5,000 more per year than you have been accustomed to paying in an area where you rarely used your heater and didn't even have air conditioning. If your real estate agent is not willing to help you get this information, it is a warning sign.

8. *What inspections do I need to have?* As a general rule, you should always get an independent home inspection. The inspector should belong to the American Society of Home Inspectors (ASHI) or one of the other national associations. In many

areas, you also need a pest inspection, or if topography is an issue, a soils inspection as well. Also make sure that the property lines are well documented. If they are not or, worse, if there is a dispute, you should insist that the seller pay for and produce a survey.

9. *What are the barriers to reselling this house?* You may be excited to make your purchase *today*, but what will your investment look like *five years* from today? There are pros and cons to neighborhood expansions; while the neighborhoods change and evolve, new highways, schools, and shopping centers must be built as well. That empty lot behind your backyard could be the next Wal-Mart Supercenter! Your realtor needs to check and provide to you all of the potential zoning changes that could have a negative impact on the house's value or the resell of your home.

## Home Buying Budget Busters

The worst outcome in buying a home is to discover—after you close—that your expenses in the new home are far higher than you expected and perhaps even over your budget. This happens all too often and can lead people down a path to foreclosure. The problem can be avoided with a little research.

The biggest budget busters are:

1. *High utility costs.* If you don't research utility costs in advance, you may be surprised—especially if you are moving to a climate with seasonal extremes. As a homeowner, all of your normal costs—maintenance, for example—are going up, but if you are surprised by the level of utility costs, you could find yourself in a real budget squeeze. A $200,000 house with a $300 utility bill will cost you less than a $175,000 house with a $600 utility bill. It's all about the net outflow of cash.

Always ask for copies of utility bills for the past year. Buying your "perfect" home without calculating all these costs will be a very expensive mistake.

2. *Unexpected bumps in property taxes.* Some states base property tax assessment on periodic estimates of values in each neighborhood. This is very informal. In some states, assessors often just drive up to homes looking for anything unusual and, if nothing is found, homes in the area are re-assessed at a higher rate than in the past. The amount of increase often is dictated by the city's or county's budget demands, more so than to reflect real market values of homes. An exception to this general rule of thumb: Some states reassess homes as soon as a sale is closed, with the new assessed value equal to the sales price. In these areas, you cannot simply look at a listing and assume that last year's property taxes are going to remain unchanged. The increase could be substantial, especially if the current owner has lived there for a long time or is paying a reduced rate (some states reduce property taxes for senior citizens, for example).

3. *Homeowner's insurance shock.* How much is your annual homeowner's insurance going to cost? A swimming pool might seem like a nice luxury, but, before getting excited, ask your homeowners insurance agent to give you a quote with a pool added. Be ready for a shock. Your premium is going to be much greater.

Remember that homeowners' insurance renews every year, meaning you are subject to increases annually. You might be in for a surprise, and you need to shop around to compare rates. After a couple of years with high claims in Mississippi and Louisiana due to devastating hurricanes a few years back (remember Katrina and Rita?), many residents in those states and neighboring states were shocked when their homeowner's insurance bill doubled or even tripled. If you check rates for national companies, you will find that rates are higher even in states without a history of disasters, because the insurer needs to spread its claims experience among *all* of its policyholders. Insurers operating only in your state may have much lower premiums for the same coverage. In other words, you need to shop around to make sure you get the best coverage for the least cost.

4. *Unexpectedly high homeowner's association dues.* If you are going to buy a home in a condominium development or even a neighborhood with a Home Owners' Association (HOA), you need to do some research ahead of time. What are the annual costs? How often have they been raised? Are there any deferred repairs that are going to require higher dues in the future? How many members are delinquent in their dues? All of these questions have to be asked to assess the real added cost of joining the association (which is mandatory). Some mixed-use HOA arrangements are unfair to some portions of the members. For example, if the HOA includes both home-owners and condo owners, what are the relative costs assessed to each? Do the bylaws specify how future cost increases are spread between the two groups?

5. *Added commute costs.* Depending on the distance between home and work, you might have to pay much higher commuting costs because of your move. Check into this and find out how much more per month you will have to pay for a rapid transit system fare or, if none is available, for driving into work (including gas, wear and tear on your car and higher insurance rates, bridge and tunnel tolls, and parking). Depending on where you live and work, commuting can be a major monthly expense. When gas prices are high, I have seen people having to sell their homes just to move closer to work, in order to afford their commutes.

## Buyer Beware

In this chapter, I have covered some of the most important considerations you need to think about when buying a home. Of course there is much more involved in deciding where to live, what you can afford, and what defines a safe and high-quality investment versus a more affordable but less desirable one. Everyone who is going to buy a home should look into all aspects of the city or town, the neighborhood and the specific property before making an offer. I have focused on the three areas I think are the ones where the greatest and most expensive mistakes are made: financing, real estate professionals, and home budgets.

In the next chapter, the even more troubling question of losing your home to foreclosure is addressed. This is a painful and frightening possibility that millions of Americans have had to face in recent years. But there are ways to reduce the expense and burden of going through foreclosure.

# CHAPTER

# 8

# What If I Lose My Castle?

W e'd all like to think that it could never happen to us—foreclosure only happens to other people. It only happens to people who made poor choices or just don't work hard enough. But this couldn't be further from the truth. To illustrate this point, I'd like to introduce you to Ryan and Kelly.

A hard-working couple in Southern California with a beautiful home and great jobs, they had purchased their home for $400,000 with a $40,000 down payment in 2006, two years before I met them. They felt very secure in every aspect of their lives, and the future only looked brighter when Ryan was offered a promotion at work. The position Ryan had aspired to and had studied so hard to some-day achieve had become available. Ryan and Kelly celebrated this wonderful news and were thrilled at the fact that the new position offered a $50,000 increase in his current salary *plus* the potential for bonuses. The only downside was that they would be moving their family to Dallas from California to take the position. This was okay, they decided, since the cost of living in Texas was consider-ably lower, so the higher income would go even further.

After coming to the realization that the transfer was inevitable, they contacted their real estate agent to get their house listed for sale. Both of them felt as though the wind was knocked out of them when the agent provided their comparative market analysis—a tool used to determine how much their home is likely to sell for. The house they had paid $400,000 for two years prior was now valued at $280,000—at best. The housing market-slump had taken its toll on the area, and they were faced with four options—all of them unthinkable.

Option #1: Don't accept the promotion—stay in California and weather the economic slump. The value in their home was likely to come back eventually.

Option #2: Take the job and move, but rent the house out for less than the mortgage payment and risk further depreciation.

Option #3: Have the agent negotiate with the mortgage company to take less than the amount owed—a short sale, which would ruin the couple's credit.

Option #4: Let the bank foreclose on the property, also a damaging blow to their credit.

Ryan and Kelly had no idea which of these scenarios would be the least devastating. They were all bad. It was a shame to see a hardworking couple who had made good choices painted into a corner like that.

As excited as you probably were to buy your very first home, an equal degree of dread is going to be fixed on the threat of losing that home. The process of *foreclosure* not only means you have to move and give up your home; it also affects your credit score for many years, often more significantly than bankruptcy.

In this chapter, I provide you with potential solutions for fixing the problem before it is too late by bringing your late payments up to date and staying in good status with your lender. But when this is not possible, you may also consider a short sale (getting the lender to accept less than the balance owed to avoid foreclosure) or even bankruptcy as alternatives to losing your home.

## Foreclosure Basics

Exactly what is foreclosure? Basically, it's a process that starts if a lender is not able to get a mortgagor (borrower) to make timely payments. Your home is security for the loan. This means that if you fail to make your payments, the lender has a legal right to take the property away from you to satisfy the obligation. If this seems obvious, you should also know that many, many home buyers do *not* understand this basic concept. Today, many people believe—wrongly—that they are entitled to a home and to home ownership, and that if they cannot make their mortgage payments, lenders have no right to kick them out. Time for a reality check: When you sign a deed of trust or mortgage, you agree to the terms, including using the property as security for the loan. This is the only protection the lender has in the event that you cannot afford the monthly payments. It's a hard reality, but it's reality nonetheless.

**911 SECRETS**

Always remember, when you sign on the dotted line to finance your home, you are agreeing to a legal obligation.

When a lender takes a home away from someone due to default, it repossesses the home, meaning it evicts a family from the property so that it can try to sell it to someone else to minimize their loss. In the same way, lien holders other than primary lenders can also force payment by placing liens on homes. These lien holders can include second mortgage lenders, contractors, home owners' associations (HOAs), individuals winning court judgments, and federal or state tax agencies.

*Foreclosure by judicial sale* is the formal name for most foreclosures. This can be filed in every state and involves the sale of property for the lender to get all or part of the balance owed. If any equity is left over after costs, the original borrower/homebuyer will get those proceeds. This is also a court-ordered legal proceeding, and the costs can be quite high, so even if you have equity in your home, by the time the process has been completed, a lot of that equity will be used up by legal fees and costs.

To decide how much is payable under foreclosure, lenders use *acceleration*. Under this process, the lender declares the entire debt to be in default, so that it is immediately due and payable under the contract's terms (the debt is accelerated and repayment demanded immediately). This debt will also include unpaid property taxes and accumulated interest and late fees, in addition to the outstanding balance on the loan. Acceleration clauses are included on the vast majority of mortgages. The lender—or, when property is sold within the procedure of foreclosure itself, the new buyer of the property—next orders the original borrower to vacate the home. If necessary, an eviction is filed so that the occupant can be legally required to leave.

Because it is possible that many unknown liens might exist on foreclosed property, the primary lender normally orders a title search and is then required to notify all people, agencies, or companies with liens. This due process gives junior lien holders the opportunity to appear in a court proceeding if applicable, or to file a claim asserting their rights. If a federal lien (usually held by the IRS) applies, the primary lender is required to file 25 days' notice of a pending sale. If this is not done, then the IRS lien stays with the property and its new owner, even after the sale has closed. (So if you ever buy a property in a foreclosure sale, you need to get your own title search even if the original lender tells you that the property search was conducted.)

A person who has been notified of a foreclosure by the lender can ask the court for a temporary injunction. The person can also challenge the validity of the debt by claiming that the lender is not a valid party to the original obligation, and thus the debt is claimed to be invalid. If this seems like a far-fetched idea, you should know that such actions have been successful in recent years and in some states.

It's more likely that if you go through foreclosure, your home is going to be repossessed and sold, perhaps through an auction. Depending on the strength or weakness of real estate in your area, the auction price might be lower than the debt level. If you do not carry private mortgage insurance (PMI) insurance (required by lenders, usually when equity is lower than 20 percent of the sales price), does this mean the lender is simply out of luck? No. It is likely that when the sale price of an auctioned or resold property does not cover the debt, they will go back to court and file for a deficiency judgment against you. This places a lien on any other property you own (or buy in the future) and obligates you to repay the difference to the lender. The deficiency would apply, however, only if the mortgage is a recourse debt (meaning the lender is entitled to sue for the deficiency). Many owner-occupied residential loans in the United States are nonrecourse, meaning the lender cannot go after you once foreclosure has been completed. However, even if your first mortgage was nonrecourse, it is possible that a refinanced mortgage or equity line of credit are recourse loans; in these cases, lenders can (and will) try to collect all of the money owed. If you end up not having to repay a deficiency, the amount could be federally taxable to you (this rule was suspended by President George W. Bush on deficiencies through 2012, but check the current rules).

## Avoiding Foreclosure

The process of foreclosure is daunting and stressful, of course, but many people can avoid having to go through it by taking preventive steps.

**911 SECRETS** Don't just walk away from your home. Always consider the many possible ways you can avoid foreclosure.

1. *Get in touch with your lender if you are having problems.* Once you realize that you are not going to be able to keep up your payment schedule, the first step you should take is to get in touch with your lender. This is counterintuitive. Many people fear that a lender, upon hearing that you are having trouble, will immediately file foreclosure. This is not true. If you get in touch before you are late on any payments, you have a better-than-average chance of finding a cooperative ear and constructive alternatives. Don't ignore the problem, hoping it will go away on its own. The majority of people who go into default have made no contact with the lender, so an aura of distrust defines the confrontational nature of the process. By expressing your desire to keep your home and to work with your lender to develop alternatives, you have a good chance of coming out of the difficult times intact. Remember, the lender does not want to foreclose. Often there is no choice because the borrower is avoiding contact.

2. *Refinance for an extended period or a lower rate.* When you talk to your lender, look for rational and practical alternatives. If your problem stems from the increased rate in an adjustable-rate loan, find out if your lender is willing to reduce your rate and move you to a fixed-rate mortgage. You can reduce payments by extending the repayment plan—in other words, starting over with a 30-year plan—which increases your long-term interest expense but also helps you to keep your home.

   If your current lender cannot help you, consider asking other lenders if they can help you refinance your present loan. Do this *before* you fall behind in your current mortgage payments. It is much easier to get a new loan if you have never been behind in your payments.

3. *Bring the account current by tapping other resources.* You should want to avoid foreclosure if at all possible. Your home is the biggest purchase you are likely make in your life, and it is also your most important asset, one worth preserving if possible. Consider all available alternatives. Tap your 401(k)

retirement fund either through a withdrawal or as collateral for a loan. Talk to family members. If you are due for a good-sized inheritance in a few years, your parents might also be willing to help you with a loan or gift today. Also consider talking to your employer. If you have a track record as a responsible employee who is valuable to the organization, your employer might also be willing to make a loan to you.

These steps make sense only if you can see how a revised plan will allow you to keep your home and also keep your financial head above water. But if, realistically, going further into debt only delays the inevitable, don't ask others to help you, and don't tap into your retirement account. Be sure you have a realistic plan for repaying borrowed money and that your plan makes sense.

4. *Ask about loan modification as an alternative to defaulting.* Many people have found themselves in a position where their loan balance is higher than their home's market value. This negative equity is very difficult to contend with because, at the time, it might seem that there is just no way out other than walking away. But there might be another path worth following. If you live in an area where values have fallen, you might be a good candidate for a loan modification. Before asking for a modification, you should know that this can adversely affect your credit rating. As part of your inquiry, ask your lender how modifying your loan's balance and terms will affect your credit.

Loan modification has become popular now that the subprime crises and accompanying housing bubble have become realities. Many lenders have had to face the difficult task of foreclosing on record high numbers of homes or agreeing to modification as a somewhat less expensive step. A modified loan with a lower interest rate or even a temporary suspension of interest payments helps homeowners keep their homes during a tough period (such as unemployment or underemployment, for example). An even more drastic step includes reducing the amount of loan that is due along with lower interest rates, in order to reduce the monthly payment. The intention of loan modification is to avoid foreclosure. The lender does not want the expense of having to foreclose and resell homes, and in comparison the cost of loan modification could be a better choice for them. A 2009 study by the Federal Reserve Bank of Boston revealed that only 3 percent of delinquent homeowners received a loan modification.*

Some lenders will play hardball, thinking they can make more profit by foreclosing and selling, but in markets with a glut of depreciated homes, that is not always the case. In such markets, it doesn't hurt to ask for a modification. Banks may resist negotiating loan modification due to the profit motive, but once the market situation gets worse in an area, they will be more likely to consider this alternative.

5. *Rent out the home.* If rental income will cover your mortgage, property tax, and insurance costs, or most of it, this could be a very practical solution that also helps you stay current on your mortgage payments. There may also be tax benefits, so talk to a certified public accountant (CPA) about the pros and cons of using your home as a rental property Be sure to take into account all of the responsibilities that come with being a landlord, and don't forget to screen your potential tenants carefully, including their credit report.

6. *Talk to a real estate professional about selling your home.* If all else fails, don't just let your lender foreclose. The damage this does to your credit is severe, and it makes it much more difficult to ever buy a home again. You may consider just biting the bullet and selling your home, regrouping, and waiting for the right time to buy again.

---

* Manuel Adelino, Kristopher Gerardi, and Paul S. Willen, "Why Don't Lenders Renegotiate More Home Mortgages? Redefaults, Self-Cures, and Securitization," Federal Reserve Bank of Boston, July 6, 2009.

Evaluate your equity in the home to determine whether selling is a viable option. In any event, do not walk away from equity unless you are hopelessly underwater. Even then, consider all of the alternatives first.

7. *Consider a short sale.* This is a solution in which your real estate agent negotiates with the lender to accept as "payment in full" an amount below the current balance of your loan. In this situation, you must ensure that the agent you're working with is skilled and experienced in negotiating short sales. Simply put, the agent who helped you into your home might not be the right guy for a short sale.

One Saturday morning, a gentleman named Mike called into my radio show. He was angry about his position, and very afraid to lose his home. Due to a combination of circumstances including a weak real estate market, the loss of a job, and uncovered medical expenses, Mike was in way over his head and facing foreclosure. I sympathized with him but also realized that he was not thinking clearly. The prospect gave him such deep anguish that he was willing to just walk away from his home rather than think through all options available to him. His delinquency was $5,000, a fraction of his stake in the home. Mike needed someone to calm him down and rationally take him through his options, and it happened that he came across my show just in time to find a beacon of light in his storm. Mike thought he had two options—walk away, or negotiate a short sale. In just a few minutes, I was able to find that Mike had a nice nest egg in a 401(k), but didn't think he was allowed to touch it before retirement. Although there are some retirement plans that won't, most of them will for the purpose of saving your homestead from foreclosure. Mike was skeptical—remember, he had already had his mind made up that there was no way out—however, he promised to call his 401(k) administrator on Monday to explore that option. It turned out that he was able to withdraw enough money from his 401(k) to bring his mortgage current and to put a little extra in savings to get him through the rough patch.

The moral of the story is this: If you are having problems keeping your mortgage payment current, foreclosure is *not* your only way out. Had Mike let his house go back or completed a short sale, it would take years for his credit to recover, not to mention the emotional toll his family would have taken as a result of losing their home. Mike, if you're out there, I hope you're doing well.

The problems with foreclosure are not just the negative hit on your credit score and the loss of your home. A couple of points that Mike and anyone else in his situation have to remember are: First, a short sale could result in your being taxed on the difference between the amount you owe and the settled amount. A moratorium was signed by President George W. Bush exempting taxation of short sales on primary residences until 2012. Second, a short sale is going to be a negative on your credit report, identified as "creditor settled for less than amount due." This is better than foreclosure, but it is still a negative that remains on your credit report for seven years.

8. *Look into bankruptcy as an alternative to foreclosure.* Talk to a bankruptcy attorney to find out what happens to your equity and to a foreclosure process if you file. The filing could delay or prevent a foreclosure. One of the first steps that occurs in a bankruptcy is that a stay is placed on any collection proceedings against you, including foreclosure (late payments and fees can be included in bankruptcy, but the principal balance cannot). The lender cannot pressure you to sell your home, refinance, or bring payments up to date until you have gone through foreclosure, which may take up to three months or more. In your discussion with the attorney, be sure that you evaluate all of the benefits and consequences of filing, not just the foreclosure issue.

Bankruptcy may also involve tax consequences depending on the terms of your filing, the type of debt, and any negotiated settlements you make with your lender and other creditors. Your credit score will fall as a consequence, and this will remain on your report for 10 years. However, as a homeowner, you are at least partially protected even if the bankruptcy court liquidates all of your assets. Every state has a *homestead* exemption for real estate. This means that the maximum homestead is protected from all creditors, even if you owe more than your equity. This does not extend to the loan you signed when you bought your home, but does exempt your equity from other lenders filing claims in bankruptcy court.

For example, in California a single person has a $50,000 exemption and married couples have $75,000 (disabled and those over 65 exempt up to $150,000). Florida, Texas, Kansas, and Oklahoma have some of the broadest homestead laws. Texas imposes no dollar value on homesteads up to 10 acres outside of a city's corporate limits. Kansas and Oklahoma has a similar rule, but it applies to up to 160 acres. You should check your state's homestead law and its limitations with your bankruptcy attorney and determine how much of your equity will actually be protected under prevailing law.

## When Foreclosure Is Inevitable

Once you have exhausted all of the possibilities, you might realize that you are simply in over your head. With little equity or even negative equity, you may not be able to find relief in any process other than foreclosure.

Know when to say "when." You can't squeeze blood from a turnip, and you might realize that in this case, you're the turnip. I'll never forget Andy and Sharon, clients who were once at the top of their financial game. Both had promising careers and plenty of income for their lifestyle, and they bought a home they thought they could afford—at least until Andy was laid off. Unfortunately, this couple also had a great deal of pride and simply didn't know when to say when. They had difficulty facing the fact that they could not afford to keep their home. They finally faced reality, though, and went through foreclosure. Oriented as they were to success, though, they got through the tragedy of their loss, regrouped themselves, and relied on their mutual love, on faith, and on their work ethic. They got their life back, as well as their good credit score, and today are back on the positive track.

As Andy and Sharon discovered, foreclosure should never be taken lightly. If it's inevitable, it has to be confronted and dealt with as soon as possible. If you end up having to go through this painful process, you are going to need to work with a skilled attorney and with a tax expert as well. Foreclosure is going to end up as one of the worst negative items you can have on your credit report, so letting this happen to you should be a very last resort. Remember too, even once you get through the foreclosure, if the lender does not get its full balance, you may find yourself named in a lawsuit for the difference. When this happens, you lose your house, your credit score plummets, and then you are sued. These reasons are why foreclosure should be the last resort.

CHAPTER

# Damage Control

Statistically speaking, one day your financial life will get turned upside down. Unfortunately, it's not a matter of *if*, but rather of *when*, you will experience an occasion that will humble you financially. There are three areas in which you are vulnerable at this very moment. I refer to these inevitable personal catastrophes as "The Three I's": insurance, investments, and identity theft. Every year, millions of people lose billions of dollars in these three areas.

## Insurance

I was in my office one Saturday morning, when Chuck and his wife came in to set up a cash-out refinance to pay off $77,000 in high-interest credit card balances they had built up in the process of furnishing their home. Chuck was a pilot for a major carrier and always on the road. When he was not traveling, Chuck collected old cars and rebuilt them. Even though he was elected the family chief financial officer (CFO), he never paid enough attention to their finances. As I was going through the paperwork, I asked to see a copy of their homeowner's insurance policy in order to structure the Good Faith Estimate.

Chuck handed it to me, and my face must have reflected my dismay as I read it. His wife asked, "What's wrong?" I said, "I've been doing this for a long time and at first glance it looks like you're paying way too much for your homeowner's insurance." I explained that we needed to immediately shop around. Chuck became visibly upset when we picked up the phone and got some quotes. He found out that he could lower his annual premium from $5,983 to $2,133 per year with exactly the same coverage—a savings of over $320 per month. He slammed his hand down on the table and said: "This is the reason we have $77,000 in credit card debt. We don't pay attention to our finances."

Chuck and his wife had overpaid almost $20,000 during the past five years. What disgusted them even more was that their agent had not taken the time to call them in over 10 years. This is one of the examples of how something as simple as an insurance policy can result in spending way too much money if you don't watch out.

## You Are at Risk

Insurance consists of two major components: rates and coverage. Losing money is a significant risk you are taking if you don't pay attention to the details.

1. *Watch out for inflated premiums.* Your insurance company probably pays out somewhere between 80 and 95 percent of all its income in claims. The Property Casualty Insurers Association of America (PCI) reported that U.S. insurers paid out 105.1 percent of premium income in 2008, compared with 95.5 percent in 2007.*

   How is this possible? A company cannot stay in business when paying out more than 100 percent of its income and even 95 percent leaves little for overhead. The answer simple. Insurance companies invest their money and make up the difference through their net investment income. Insurers are "institutional" investors (along with mutual funds and pension

---

* Ravi Nagarajan, "Berkshire's Insurance Subsidiaries Buck Property/Casualty Headwinds in 2008," *The Rational Walk*, at www.rationalwalk.com, April 10, 2009.

plans), and they have billions of dollars in the stock and bond markets. This is the point: If your insurance company has a lousy year with its investments, it has to pass on those losses to make up the difference. Guess who pays more? That's right, you do. A leading reason for inflated premiums is poor *investment* performance, often a greater cause for higher premiums than actual levels of claims filed.

Take the time to understand how insurance companies make money. You may be paying a higher premium because of their poor investments.

Of course, not all insurance companies have the same level of losses, even in a terrible year. For this reason, you need to shop around and compare rates. All insurance companies are *not* the same. In fact, you are going to find significant differences among companies for identical coverage, due to variations in investment income.

2. *Check every year to make sure you are not underinsured.* For certain types of insurance coverage, *most* people are underinsured. Even in areas that experience devastating fires every few years, such as southern California, the problem is chronic. Nationally, most—68 percent—of all homeowners carry too little homeowners' coverage.*

This results from several factors, including not keeping up with increasing property values, performing additions and renovations without upgrading policies, failing to insure jewelry or collectibles, and simply not knowing what is and is not covered. In other words, you might be underinsured

---

*Liz Pulliam Weston, "Is your home underinsured? 8 key points," *MSN Money Central,* July 14, 2009.

just because you—like most Americans—don't know what is included in your policy and what may be excluded.

## Make a Collect Call

When was the last time your agent called you? Your agent should call you at least once a year, but the truth is that most agents don't take the time to contact their existing customers. They are more interested in focusing on new business and the commission it pays them. Agents earn more commissions in the first year a policy is in force, and their rate falls off in subsequent years—a reality that generates a lot of new business but does nothing for you, the existing policyholder. Unfortunately, you probably have to make the call each year. If you do not make the call, and blindly renew your policy without checking rates, insurance agents get paid a commission based on renewals. This encourages some agents not to contact you with information regarding changes in rates.

**911 SECRETS** You need to make contact with your insurance agent once per year. Don't wait for your agent to call you.

Insist on a review of your policy annually to make sure your agent is covering all of your insurance needs, based on what you have, what it's worth, and how much deductible you are willing to pay. This process is a win-win situation because if you shop around and lower your premiums, you're putting money right in your pocket every month. Even if you discover your rates are the best available, you have the peace of mind that you're doing everything you can to save yourself money, which is an even bigger win.

When you set up a review of your policy with your agent, make sure you take these four important questions with you:

1. *Is my credit score affecting my rates?* Many insurance companies use credit scores to assess risk and determine the chances that you will file a claim, and then set rates accordingly. How does this affect your premiums? The lower the credit score, the higher the rates. If your rates have been affected by your score, shop around. There's a good chance you can get a better rate for the same coverage.

2. *Am I covered appropriately?* Go line by line through the policy with your agent, and ask the appropriate questions: "What if a storm hits my house? Or it floods? Or it's vandalized? Or I have a car accident? Am I covered and what will be my out-of-pocket expense?"

   Chances are, you do not know the answers to these questions, but you have to know. Your agent has all of these answers and can provide you with a very fast reality check. For example, many companies are able to keep your rates the same as they were last year, even though their investments performed poorly. How can they do this? They raise your deductible without informing you because it's there in the nitty-gritty of your detailed annual policy declaration.

3. *Am I receiving all the discounts I'm eligible for?* If you carry homeowners' and auto insurance with different insurance companies, find out how much discount you could get by carrying coverage with the same company for all of your needs. A multipolicy discount can save substantial amounts of money, including homeowners', auto, life, and umbrella policies. Shop for not only the best coverage, but also for the most generous discounts as well.

4. *When is the last time my company raised my rates?* If you haven't talked to your agent but your rates have gone up every year for the past five years, *why is that the case?* What changed? For example, if your premium goes up 10 percent each year, over five years, your premium has gone up 161 percent. Wouldn't it be nice if you could go to your boss every year and ask for a 10 percent raise? It would be easier if, like your insurance

company, you could write your own payroll check without talking to the boss first. That's what your insurance company may be doing, while burying the reasons in the fine print of your policy declarations.

Insurance is not an exciting topic, I know. Perhaps this is why a majority of people do not take the time to check and comparison shop. You probably spend more time comparing prices at different gas stations than for your homeowners' and auto policy rates. But when it comes to your credit, remember these important points:

- Being underinsured is a direct threat to your financial safety.
- Your credit score might be affecting what you pay.
- Not every insurer is the same, and it is always smart to shop for better rates.

The second "I"—investments—presents a completely different set of challenges to you and your financial health.

## Investments

I received an online application through my web site one morning from a woman inquiring about a refinance. As I was reviewing it, I saw that the client, Kathleen, was a financial planner, making about $175,000 a year. As I looked down at the "current interest rate" part of the form, I thought there was a typo. It said the interest rate on her mortgage was 12 percent. As I began to look over her credit, I asked myself: "How is this lady a *financial planner*? She can't even manage her own finances, let alone someone else's." Her credit report was filled with late payments, collections, and even a few repossessions. I picked up the phone to call her. When Kathleen answered, she said, "I'm sure your first question is how I am a financial planner with an interest rate at 12 percent." She took the words right out of my mouth.

As a mortgage originator, it is part of my job to look over people's entire financial picture. Every day I see people losing money with their insurance rates and coverage and also with financial planners to whom they have entrusted their money! While it's easy to love our financial planner when they're making us money, it's even easier to be furious with them when they lose our money. However, we can't simply hand over the responsibility to our own personal finances; your financial health is ultimately *your* responsibility. A typical conversation in my office goes something like this:

*Client:* My investment and retirement accounts have been losing so much value that I don't even open my statements any more.
*Me:* Where is your money invested?
*Client:* I don't know.

## Where Is Your Money?

When taking the time to secure your financial stability, keep your focus on simple, to-the-point information:

1. *Decide who is in control.* The worst situation is one in which you have no idea who is making decisions with your investment funds. You, your spouse, and a financial adviser might all play a role in picking investments, buying and selling, and even the basic definition of risk. Like three blind men trying to describe an elephant, this is not the best way to proceed. Your very first step is to appoint a chief investment officer (CIO). Just like the family chief financial officer (CFO) described earlier, the CIO has to be in control of every aspect of your family's investment decisions.

2. *Find out whether you are making or losing money.* If you don't know the answer to this, you have a 911 situation. You have to immediately perform a "financial triage" to decide if and where you are "bleeding funds" and, once identified, how to stop the bleeding—immediately. It is amazing to me that so many people will worry about how much their monthly cable bill or newspaper is costing, while their investment portfolio is in shambles. *Prioritize.* Your investments need to be in

165

products that correspond with your risk tolerance. This is a factor you need to define with your financial adviser, based on your income, experience in the markets, your age and years to target retirement date, monthly expenses, and long-term goals. No two people have the same risk tolerance.

**911 SECRETS** Don't be naive. The stock market is nothing more than legalized gambling.

3. *Figure out what you can do right now to fix the problem.* You cannot ignore your monthly statements from your brokerage firm or mutual fund just because you dread what you will find out. You need to take control of the money and make the tough decisions. Remember, this might be like first aid. You cannot ignore a patient who is bleeding, or who has stopped breathing, or who has gone into shock. I know, you think opening your monthly statement may put you in a state of shock. Believe me, ignoring the problem is not a better choice.

If you are able and willing to take care of your investments on your own, make sure you have your money in products that match your risk tolerance. You may decide to use an online discount broker, a mutual fund or family of funds, or other products. But if you conclude that you need help, you will need to hire a financial consultant or adviser. Depending on how much you understand investing, you might need someone to guide you through to the right choices, or you might need to hire someone to basically help you define your financial goals, and then recommend how to reach them.

In finding the best financial adviser, ask for referrals from trusted associates, including your attorney, tax preparer, banker, mortgage lender, and accountant. At your first meeting, which is essentially a job interview, you (as employer) need to find out how often your adviser will meet with you in person and how and when you will be able to get in touch with him. An important question is to ask how long it will take to get a return phone call after a message is left. What you *don't* need is someone who is difficult to reach and who does not return phone calls for three days.

911 SECRETS

Always put your financial planner through a job interview! It's the most important hire you will ever make.

Remembering that you are conducting the interview. Ask the adviser why you should trust him or her to assist you. What you want to hear is that the person does not simply point you to the latest hot idea. They should listen to you and develop an investment plan suitable for your risk tolerance and goals. Also ask the person for his or her personal investing strategy. Make sure you agree in principle. It is very difficult to try to get advice from someone who is continually trying to get you to move outside of your investment comfort zone (and your risk tolerance). Finally, make sure you know the full range of charges and fees involved, and how the adviser is compensated. Some financial planners get a fee only, while others work on commission. Some get both. If you are expected to pay a commission for advice, you also want to make sure that the recommendations are based on what is best for you, and not on the product yielding the highest commission.

Remember, though, that no matter how successful your investment program or adviser, all will be at risk if someone steals your identity. For this reason, the third "I"—identity theft—is equally as important as the other two.

## The Third "I"—Identify Theft

Some months ago, I had an empty-nester couple visit my office, where we excitedly discussed their options of downsizing into a nice home near the golf course. Kevin and Marie had recently sent their last kid off to college and were thrilled at the idea of keeping up a smaller house and spending their retired days playing golf.

Their purchase was contingent upon the sale of their current house, and after 120 days of waiting and hoping, they had finally received a contract on their home and were ready to move forward with their new purchase. As credit reports must be updated after 90 days, my heart dropped when I repulled their credit. "Marie," I said, extremely concerned, "your score has dropped from a 721 to a 586. You have three new credit cards reporting as 30 days late— and they've only been open for 60 days." She looked completely confused. "Rodney, I haven't opened any credit cards in over a year. I have no idea what those are."

**911 SECRETS** You are likely to have your identity stolen by a family member, friend, or someone you work with rather than a complete stranger.

After looking over her credit report, I realized she had fallen victim to identity theft, and consequently they lost their dream home. The worst part of the whole situation? The thief was her 35-year-old daughter, who had already done this once before. Should Kevin and Marie have been surprised? When it comes to identity theft committed by a relative, remember this rule: If they did it before, they are going to do it again.

In some mystical cultures, reference is made to a "third eye," which is a higher plane of consciousness. You need to be aware of a different "third I" to ensure a higher plane of *financial* consciousness, which is essential in order to prevent having your identity stolen.

## You Are Vulnerable

Some forms of theft are just so easy that you have to expect to lose. If you leave a wad of hundred dollar bills sitting out in the open, someone is eventually going to take it. By the same logic, if laws are not set up to prevent identity theft across state and international lines, it's only a matter of time until a smart crook figures out how to clean out your accounts, max out your credit cards, and even open up new cards in your name. These risks are not just theories— losses of staggering volume and proportion are taking place every day. People's credit is ruined, and it takes years to correct it. Money is lost and never replaced. Even home equity can be stolen by sophisticated con artists.

### *Before It Happens*

Identity theft is a growing problem and has been for many years. It is often perpetrated by people you know: family, friends, and co-workers. A common problem is co-workers stealing credit cards from purses left on a desk, or out of suit coats left on a hanger in the office, or from a locker. The assumption that your property is safe with co-workers can be a dangerous and costly assumption. Nearly half of all identity theft complaints involve someone the victim knows. How can you best protect yourself? First of all, know that identity theft is not always committed by strangers. Between 9 and 10 million cases are reported annually, accounting for nearly 40 percent of all complaints filed with the Federal Trade Commission, and half of all cases involve relatives, friends, and neighbors as the perpetrators.*

The 9 to 10 million figure reported in 2005 was confirmed in 2008, which saw a 22 percent increase over 2007. Low-tech methods

---

* Michelle Singletary, "When ID Theft Starts at Home," *Washington Post*, February 13, 2005.

are among the most popular, including stolen wallets and personal documents (43 percent of all identity theft). So just being extra diligent with your purse or wallet and with your paperwork is likely to prevent nearly half of all cases.

You can prevent theft by strangers by being diligent in many other ways. For example, if you leave your credit card receipt in a restaurant, a server of bus-person can easily retrieve it. Also, check your monthly statements carefully, and make sure you have not been double-billed for anything. Does this happen? Yes. One fairly elaborate scheme happened a few years ago in California was put into motion by a clerk in a retail store. He ran through a charge but made a second slip by running the card through a second time. He waited a full month and then put through the second charge as though a sale had been made for exactly the same amount. He simply put the store's copy of the charge slip into the register and removed the same amount of cash.

**911 SECRETS** Unfortunately, no one is immune to identity theft. Investing in identity theft protection is no longer a luxury; it's a necessity!

Why was this such an effective method? Most people do not check their monthly statement carefully, and only pay attention when they see a charge they don't recognize. So when the victim saw the second charge, he or she did not compare the statement to the previous month. Recalling he or she had bought something at that store, he or she simply paid the bill and never thought twice about the possibility of being charged double.

When it comes to taking your money, many thieves are creative, even ingenious.

Your information can be taken in many ways, even out of your own garbage can. With this in mind, always assume that whatever you throw away and put out at the curb immediately becomes public property. Any piece of paper with a credit card number, your date of birth, social security number, online account names and passwords, should be shredded before it is thrown away. Everyone should have a shredder in the home and use it to destroy all sensitive documents.

You also need to take preemptive steps to prevent losses in your bank account. For example, even though an insured account is protected by insurance, how long will it take your bank to put money back into your account after it is cleaned out by an identity thief? Phone your bank manager and ask for an explanation of the bank's identity theft policy. If it is going to take several days to get your stolen funds replaced, what will you do in the meantime? It could be that all of the checks you wrote will start bouncing, making the problem even worse. Not only will you start racking up fees, but all of those credit card, mortgage, utility, and other payments are bouncing—all because your bank does not put the money back in immediately.

Bank policies vary, and among the many criteria for picking one bank over another, identity theft policies should be one you use. Identity theft resolution could take years, even when you are able to explain what happened. Past-due bills don't always get cleared from your credit report right away, so you need to know how your bank handles identity theft and how long you will be without funds.

**911 SECRETS**    Always make sure your bank's identity theft rules protect you!

Even losing your cell phone can destroy your credit. If someone steals your cell phone and charges begin piling up, you are responsible until you cancel the account and get a new number. What might look like a minor inconvenience could result in your being on the hook for thousands of dollars in overseas calls placed in only a few days' time.

Prevent problems by being very protective of sensitive information. This includes your social security number, date of birth, and driver's license number. Keep all documents such as passports, birth certificates, and military discharge documents under lock and key, preferably in a safe or a safety deposit box.

## Once It Happens

After your identity has been stolen, whether limited to credit cards, cell phones, or online accounts, remember that there is no such thing as a minor or unimportant identity theft. Any information can be used to find out more, and any theft can ruin your credit.

Immediately contact all companies issuing credit cards that have been stolen. You could be responsible for all charges incurred if you do not immediately call in the stolen card number that every credit card company provides. You *must* make the call and cancel all affected cards.

Second, you need to file a police report right away. Many people don't take this step because they don't think the police will be able to find the thief. That's not the point. While you could be right about the effort being futile on the surface, the police report is an essential step. Before any negative information is removed from your credit report, the credit bureaus will require a copy of the police report. In addition, companies with charges in your name will not remove those charges until you provide them with the police report as well. The police report is a lifeline to clearing up the problem, because it validates the crime.

Contact all three credit bureaus (Equifax, Experian, and TransUnion) immediately. You must contact all three to ensure that items do not remain on any of your credit reports as a result of identity theft.

Finally, remember the story of Kevin and Marie at the beginning of this section. If someone has stolen your identity in the past, they are probably going to try to steal it again in the future. Even beloved relatives (in some cases, especially beloved relatives) cannot be trusted once they have stolen from you.

With this in mind, make a wise investment of about $100 per year, and sign up with a credit-monitoring service. Make sure the service you pay for comes with a guarantee that the company will fix any problems that come up, working on your behalf. This step truly could save your financial life. Fixing your credit after identity theft is not the end of the story. For far too many Americans every year, it is only the beginning. This is why credit monitoring is essential.

# CHAPTER 10

# Bankruptcy: Losing the Battle to Win the War

A lot of people run into financial troubles due to circumstances beyond their control. When they do, they're in good company.* Among the well-known people who have filed bankruptcy are Walt Disney, Elton John, Donald Trump, Dave Ramsey, Willie Nelson, and Henry Ford. Each and every one successfully emerged and thrived after bankruptcy. You must know when to say "when," and known when enough is enough. If you earn $40,000 a year, and you have $80,000 in credit card debt, the chances of your ever getting out from under this debt are slim to none. Bankruptcy protection is there for the situations that need it. Even General Motors and Chrysler found themselves in the position where bankruptcy was the best option. Medical expenses beyond any health insurance coverage, loss of a job, or even an expensive divorce can all lead to bankruptcy. The stigma associated with the process makes it more painful than it should be. For many, bankruptcy is like a big sign hung around the neck and reading "failure."

---

* Many of the suggestions, ideas, and guidelines in this chapter were generously provided by attorney Reed Allmand, author of *The Truth about Bankruptcy* (2009).

"Failure is the opportunity to start over more intelligently."

—Henry Ford

This does not have to be the case. If you are thinking about filing bankruptcy, you should certainly make sure it is the only choice available. But if you do, there is no reason why you cannot survive the process and get the "fresh start" that you're entitled to as part of discharging your debts. It will take time and diligence to rebuild your credit, but you—like millions of others—can do it. Often there is simply no other choice. In this chapter, I am going to cover the essential steps you need to go through first. Do you need to file bankruptcy? What types of filings are available? What are the steps? What happens after you file?

There are many half-truths, myths, and downright untruths associated with bankruptcy. Even with widespread accurate information available, these misleading beliefs persist. Hopefully, the information in this chapter will be enlightening for you and will provide you with an accurate view of how the entire process works.

## What Exactly Is Bankruptcy?

Among the reasons for the negative stigma attached to the idea of bankruptcy is the history behind it. Today we have come a long way from the debtors' prisons of the sixteenth century.

The word *bankruptcy* is derived from two Latin words, *bancus* (a counter used by merchants) and *ruptus* ("broken"). In old Rome, anyone who was not able to pay their taxes could be removed from their business and replaced by a trustee to ensure that back taxes would eventually be paid. Properties were auctioned and sold by the trustee, who also determined which creditors received payment.

176

The first modern bankruptcy laws were put into place in England in the sixteenth century during the age of King Henry VIII. Considering the fact that this was a king who would behead his own wife, those falling on financial hard times had no to reason to expect mercy. People unable to pay their debts were likely to be sent to debtors' prison, where their entire family also accompanied them. The change from prison to forgiveness often is assumed to be a sign of a more enlightened view of debt problems. The truth, though, is that the first bankruptcy laws were passed because the debtors' prisons were full. The system wasn't working. Under the first laws, some debts could be discharged, but creditors could continue to try and collect even after the filing. Bankruptcy trustees were even allowed to forcibly break into debtors' homes and take property.

911 SECRETS
Modern bankruptcy laws were designed to help you —not hurt you.

It may have seemed like progress to do away with prison, but the strong-arm practices of trustees were at times just as unpleasant. Debtors could be publicly ridiculed by being displayed in a pillory, having an ear cut off, or even being nailed to a slab of wood. Nasty stuff—but it explains how the disgrace and failure associated with bankruptcy had its roots in some very real public sentiments toward those who were not able to pay their debts. Today, debtors are not usually nailed up or publicly displayed, but the disgrace often remains. It was not until nearly halfway through the nineteenth century that a federal bankruptcy law was passed in the United States that began the modern process. A depression hit the country in 1837 and a few years later, in 1841, Congress set up the system still in place today. For the first time, individuals were allowed to file bankruptcy rather than the older system, in which creditors filed bankruptcy *against* someone as a method for getting payment. That law was repealed in 1843 after a constitutional challenge, and was not replaced until a new law in 1867. This was also repealed, in 1878.

If it seems that these laws were passed after economic hard times and then repealed during periods of recovery, you're right. The economy turned downward once again in 1893, which led to the Bankruptcy Act of 1898. This law remained in effect until the modern day, with major changes made in 1938, 1978, and 2005. These overhauls fine-tuned the legislation and have continued a philosophical change. Bankruptcy is no longer meant as a form of punishment or retribution, but as an orderly system for discharging debts that people cannot afford to pay.

One important concept within this legal and philosophical body of law is that of the *fresh start*. For whatever reason, a person or company who was not able to pay their obligations is discharged in a bankruptcy proceeding. The sale of assets may provide partial relief to creditors, and the petitioner's credit rating is going to be lowered at least for a while. In a process that seems dark, drastic, and hopeless, the person is entitled to a fresh start; another chance to restore good credit and financial health. It is quite a leap from sending whole families to debtors' prison.

## Do You Really Need to File for Bankruptcy Protection?

Bankruptcy is not a punishment. In fact, it is not an admission of failure either. True, a person who has to file due to a gambling problem or addiction to drugs or alcohol has certainly suffered from either a character flaw or a disease. However, many people have had to file bankruptcy because their medical bills have overwhelmed them even when they thought they had the right insurance. In other cases, their jobs were taken from them and no suitable replacements were available, or they were underemployed as one aspect of economic hard times. In other words, associating bankruptcy with some kind of character flaw, sin, or weakness is simply unfair. However, deciding whether you need to file bankruptcy first requires that you know what the process is and how it works.

**911 SECRETS**  A bankruptcy is not a punishment. It is a solution to real-life problems.

Start by evaluating your *current* financial health and answer these questions:

1. *Do you live paycheck to paycheck?* Anyone who just barely makes it from one check to another is at great risk. If you are laid off, your car breaks down, or if a child becomes ill, it's likely that you are going to be underwater financially. Living paycheck to paycheck is continual, stressful form of living with never-ending risk.

2. *Do you pay bills late as a matter of routine?* In spite of what some people believe, once you start falling behind on your bills, the problem only worsens. You don't magically or suddenly catch up. Those late payments just get later and later, and you get a growing number of "past due" bills in pink or red envelopes, followed by threats to consign your debt to collection or to take other legal action. Then the phone calls begin, and your credit is completely ruined.

3. *Do you overdraw your checking account regularly?* If you do not write down your transactions, you really have no idea how much money is in your account. In this situation, you are going to overdraw your account, and perhaps frequently. You cannot go online and check what the bank says you have on hand, because that balance does not include any checks you

wrote recently that have not yet cleared. Not knowing your balance and not writing down your transactions is a very self-destructive habit. You need to fix this problem and begin a diligent program of tracking your money to avoid overdrawing your account.

4. *Are all of your credit cards maxed out?* The truth is, if you have used up all of your credit, you are living beyond your means and it's only downhill from this point on. Take control of your credit and figure out how to self-discipline so that this kind of problem is brought under control.

5. *Are you being assessed late fees and over-limit fees on your credit card accounts?* If your monthly statement includes those nasty extra fees, it's a further red flag telling you that you are out of control. Many credit card companies make the situation worse by increasing your credit limit. However, we all know that soon after this happens, you once again find yourself maxed out. Chances are, you are using those cards to buy big-screen TVs, backyard grills, or expensive vacations. If so, you need to do a reality check. The short-term gratification has a price, and that is long-term financial self-destruction.

The poor financial habits described in the preceding points are typical of people who have never applied financial self-discipline. Part of the problem is lack of education for people entering the world of credit, but the larger part is a cultural and social tendency to live beyond our means and to push the problem forward instead of solving it.

**911 SECRETS** Living beyond your means is one of the quickest paths into bankruptcy court.

There are four primary reasons that people file bankruptcy. These are:

1. *Medical bills.* The medical and health insurance systems in this country are in terrible shape, and there are many theories as to why. But the worst situation within this problem is that many people, including those with medical insurance, find themselves rather quickly in trouble when a major hospital visit is needed or when disease strikes. Uninsured people cannot be turned away and care will be provided; however, the bill has to be paid. Those with insurance may be told by their insurers that a specific problem is not covered, and, even for covered incidents, dollar limits on insurance claims, deductibles, and copayments often mean that after insurance is paid, you are left with a huge debt.

2. *Divorce.* No one thinks that divorce is cheap or easy. For the majority of people going through it, the combination of legal fees, loss of retirement accounts, destruction of investments and savings, ongoing alimony and child support, and declining credit scores can easily start a downhill process in which a once-solvent family turns into two warring sides, with one or both destitute. The divorce system in the United States is horrible and destructive, and many divorce attorneys who perpetrate the negative aspects of divorce often keep the proceedings going as long as there are assets remaining to be destroyed as a part of the process.

3. *Job loss.* When the unemployment rate moved from about 5 percent in 2006 up to over 10 percent by 2010, millions of American families were devastated. Unable to continue mortgage payments, people were forced into foreclosure, and the stress worsened on families as bread winners were unable to find work for an extended period. As unemployment compensation ran out, the situation became desperate for many. The official unemployment numbers don't even count those who

have simply given up, and, at the time when unemployment was over 10 percent in 2009, the real number was above 17 percent. For many, bankruptcy was the inevitable outcome of losing a job and remaining unemployed for many months, even years.

4. *High and growing debt.* Finally, many people allow their debt levels to rise over time. The debt level is simply too high for the level of income, and it becomes impossible to ever recover. When every spare nickel is going toward minimum payments on a number of credit cards, getting the debt paid off can become impossible. At that point, the person may be forced to consider bankruptcy.

In any of these circumstances, bankruptcy should be the path of last resort. No one should ever proceed lightly and without first trying to get debts under control. If you are left with no other choice, you are entitled to bankruptcy protection.

## What Type of Bankruptcy Should You File?

There are three different classifications of bankruptcy, and each is designed to work for a particular group. The first of these, and the most popular for individuals, is Chapter 7 bankruptcy. Under this version, most unsecured debts can be discharged without a requirement for repayment. However, the bankruptcy court does require that many assets be sold to repay a portion of the debt. After 2005, guidelines tightened, making it more difficult to qualify for a Chapter 7 filing. The bankruptcy court has the right to determine whether a person is qualified, and may require taking a different route. It has become much more difficult for people to discharge credit card debt under the rules put in place in 2005.

A second bankruptcy option is a Chapter 13 bankruptcy. This is a debt consolidation plan allowing the individual to restructure debt and repay it over a period of time, as long as five years in many cases. The court may even suspend interest on the debt. They require that a person's income be adequate to afford the required repayment schedule. Included in the repayment may be late mortgage interest (but not principal), auto loans, medical bills, installment debt, and credit card balances. The court sets the monthly payment based on debt levels and income.

The third bankruptcy classification is Chapter 11, which is also a form of debt reorganization, but reserved for businesses. It is similar to Chapter 13 and may be used to save a struggling business at risk of failing.

In any of these situations, you need to consult with a qualified attorney to determine:

- What type of bankruptcy is most advantageous for you?
- What type of protection are you qualified to seek?
- How does one choice or the other affect your credit in coming years?

## What Steps Do You Need to Take?

It is important to explore every option available to you and every facet of bankruptcy, should this be the best avenue for you. Consult with a qualified financial planner as well and make sure you have no choice but to file for bankruptcy. If this is the inescapable conclusion, the first thing you need to do is to find an attorney.

Why check with a financial expert first? If you go right to a bankruptcy attorney, you may or may not get good advice. Asking an attorney if you *need* an attorney is at times like asking a used car salesman if you need to buy a car. You need an objective evaluation of your situation as a starting point.

Finding a qualified bankruptcy attorney can be tedious and discouraging. Many grind out hundreds of filings per month and know exactly what they are doing for the *typical* situation. But if you have any complex problems, you may need to pay extra for a higher level of expertise. For example, if you own any business interests or intellectual properties (such as royalty rights to a book), a run-of-the-mill bankruptcy attorney might not know exactly how the law works. The ugly truth is that *many* of your intellectual and investment properties can (and will) be sold by the trustee in a Chapter 7 filing. Special situations like that can be disastrous if the *typical* assumptions are applied in atypical situations.

 You must start re-establishing credit as soon as your bankruptcy is discharged.

John was a writer. He filed for Chapter 7 protection when the economy turned sour and he was no longer able to keep ahead of his growing credit card balances. He hesitantly hired a bankruptcy attorney who assured him that the process was fast, simple and automatic. However, after the discharge of debts, the trustee informed the attorney that he was going to sell *all* of the author's royalties for books written before the filing date. This wiped out over 20 years of building a career. It was devastating. The attorney was taken by surprise *himself*. He had no idea that intellectual properties were subject to liquidation in bankruptcy. This attorney claimed to have completed hundreds of filings, but he simply did not know the law. The worst part of the entire agonizing process was that the trustee ended up selling the royalty stream to the author's ex-wife.

To find a *qualified* attorney, you have to make a good match. If you do not have any investments or unusual properties and are just seeking a straightforward discharge, you can probably use a high-volume service. However, just as you need good financial advice when going through a divorce, you *must* have sound financial advice when filing bankruptcy. It is unlikely that a bankruptcy attorney also understands taxes, financial planning, and property issues. You either need to get high-level advice first, or find an attorney who is qualified to advise you in every area.

Choosing the wrong attorney can also lead to problems within the filing itself. For example, if you do not properly list exemptions, leave off some accounts in your list of assets, reaffirm existing debts, or file improperly, you could find yourself in noncompliance, putting the entire process at risk. If your attorney is not diligent in making sure that the process is done completely and thoroughly, you could find yourself unable to meet the requirements or filing deadlines. This is why a high-volume attorney is not the best choice in every case, and may be appropriate only for the most basic, simple, and straightforward filings.

When choosing an attorney, here are a few sources available to you:

1. *The yellow pages.* This is probably the worst place to start your search. Any lawyer can buy an ad in the phone book, and this provides you with no system for comparing qualifications.
2. *Referrals from family or friends.* This may be a way to go, but you cannot be sure. Ask not only for the name, but also for the reasons your source considers the attorney to be a good choice for you.
3. *Referrals from another attorney.* This is a good choice, assuming that the attorney is a trusted adviser. Preferably, it should be a person who has advised you on financial issues in the past and who has explored other options with you as a first step.
4. *The state or local bar association.* The options you find here are unlikely to be completely unbiased. Generally, they will not criticize their own members, and even when complaints are filed against attorneys, they may not be disclosed on the association's web site. The referral you get from the bar will only be a member in close proximity that specializes in bankruptcy, not necessarily the most qualified, best, or complaint-free choice.

Your list of initial questions in deciding which attorney to hire should include:

- How many filings do you do in a year? (Remember, more is not always better.)
- How many of those cases have you successfully taken through to final discharge of debts? (Look for a high percentage.)

- What percentage of your Chapter 13 filings are confirmed? (Again, you want to see a high percentage here.)
- Will you handle my case personally, or will the bulk go to a paralegal or legal secretary? (In the case of the writer cited previously, when he showed up at court, the attorney was nowhere to be seen. He sent his secretary—not even a *legal* secretary—to file the papers for him.)
- How often will you give me updates on my status? (A good attorney will keep you updated regularly on the progress of your petition.)
- What is your fee, and what does it include? (Some bankruptcy attorneys charge a flat fee for all services through final discharge, but may charge additional fees for further services.)

## How Does the Process Begin?

When you hire the bankruptcy attorney, he or she first asks you to sign a retainer agreement and to make your payment. Once this takes place, your first interview occurs and should include an evaluation of your case and your financial situation. This is a defining step, during which the attorney is supposed to provide you with your choices and explain the pros and cons of each.

911 SECRETS

Always make sure that your bankruptcy attorney explains the items that can and cannot be included in your bankruptcy case.

You should bring with you to this interview: copies of your latest credit reports, all of your most recent credit card statements, your mortgage statement, your income documentation, and current bank account statements. Also, bring your investment account monthly statement, if applicable. In other words, bring along *all* of your credit-related documents.

Your attorney should review all of your documents and explain how you should proceed. The decision about what kind of bankruptcy protection to seek should be based on your income, debt levels, and the types of debts. The attorney should then explain to you all of the legal issues and draw up the itemized filing documents.

Once all of the official forms are filled out and signed, you are expected to file the petition with the court. Chances are, you will also be required to provide between one and three years of tax returns as part of your petition. In a Chapter 13, the next step is called the meeting of creditors. This phase provides the chance for any of your creditors to file objections to the process, and also gives the trustee a chance to determine what is to be included or excluded in the bankruptcy filing. After this, the court reaffirms all of your debts by sending notification to all creditors, including deadlines for the final discharge. At the same time, a stay is put in place so that creditors are banned from continuing collection efforts, contacting you, and even sending out monthly statements.

## The Advantage of Taking Action Early

Many people file bankruptcy only when their situation has become disastrous. In other words, creditors are calling and making threats, collection agencies are on the case, and you are receiving past due notices daily. If you know you are heading down this path, seeking bankruptcy protection early on is better. If you have made monthly payments on time without fail on credit card and mortgage accounts, but you can see that your balances are growing and there is no other way out, now is the time to begin preliminary talks and seek guidance from a qualified bankruptcy attorney.

It is even possible to file for bankruptcy protection without ever having a late payment on your record. If you move early—advised when there really is no other choice—it is actually possible to have the bankruptcy as the only negative item on your credit report. In this case, it is substantially easier to rebuild your good name and takes less time. The paradox of filing bankruptcy while also having excellent credit is not at all farfetched. In fact, if you know you are eventually going to be forced to make this choice, it is a rational decision to file early, rather than later when you are past due on all of your accounts.

**911 SECRETS**

Bankruptcy is not a financial death sentence; it's simply losing the battle to win the war.

The idea of filing bankruptcy is taboo in our culture. While, in some cases, it is a completely responsible and precautious step to *avoid* financial disaster, feelings of failure and hopelessness are often present. The best way to survive the experience is to recognize that going through bankruptcy does not make you a bad person or always lead to an unsuccessful future. It makes you one of the millions who have fallen under the financial bus during a difficult economic time. Many of those who would judge you negatively for going through bankruptcy might themselves be only one paycheck away from financial ruin. You are not alone.

I have taken you through many painful topics in the previous chapters: credit card problems, poorly vetted marriage, expensive divorce, collections, risks of buying real estate with the wrong expert help, foreclosure, and bankruptcy. These are the worst things that can happen to you and, short of ill health or the death of a loved one, they are the most devastating experiences a person can have. Know, also, that there are steps you can take to not only avoid these problems, but also to save your financial life during and after these negative experiences. In the next chapter, I conclude with some last words of advice and a summary of the financial defensive measures you can take today to ensure long-lasting financial health.

# CHAPTER 11

# Saving Your Financial Life

There has been a lot of doom and gloom in this book, out of necessity. I have had to talk about things you might not have known about, but that affect you nonetheless. Worse still, I may have put words before you revealing truths you already knew but were afraid to confront. If that's the case, you are not alone.

Let me say it again: *You are not alone.*

In the United States, the most prosperous country in the world and perhaps in history, we face a paradox. We are largely a financially illiterate population. So many people fail financially every year, and for many reasons. Most common among these are larger systemic failures in our families and schools. As a country, we do not educate our children and students in financial matters. Many kids coming out of high school do not know anything about checking accounts, credit cards, or financial planning. If they know anything, it is that when they go away to college, Dad and Mom are going to give them their own credit card. Cool.

There is little value in assigning blame. It's bad enough when someone's credit is destroyed, when they marry the wrong person, or when they go through divorce, foreclosure, or bankruptcy. To blame someone else is a way of avoiding responsibility, but to blame yourself is equally nonproductive. The point is: Now you need to change how things were in the past. You need to rebuild your credit, fix the problems and habits that contributed to the problem, and begin all over with a new perspective on money and credit.

If you are to have any chance for a successful future, you do need to take a harsh and realistic look at the habits of the past. In previous chapters I have shown you the questions you need to ask and the steps you have to take to (a) avoid problems before they hit you, (b) mitigate the loss from what's happening right now, and (c) prevent those problems from recurring in the future. You don't get a recovering alcoholic a job as a bartender, and you don't expect a recovering gambler to work in a casino. These people have to avoid temptation as part of their recovery process. By the same argument, you are going to need to change the habits that led to past problems.

If one of your problems was abusing credit cards, it doesn't really help you to shun using credit cards forever, but it does make sense to set new rules for yourself. For example, your rules may include:

- Any use of a credit card is going to be limited to what I can afford to pay off every month.
- No balances will be carried forward except emergencies. In the event of an emergency, I will immediately stop using my credit card until its balance is paid down to zero, even if that means tightening my budget drastically.
- Even when I get attractive offers, I will not take low-interest transfers on my cards for any purpose. I acknowledge that credit cards are not meant for this. No longer will I believe that "a penny borrowed is a penny earned." Now I know that "a penny borrowed compounds to a dollar *owed*."
- I limit my credit cards to two or three at the most, and will not apply for more credit even when the offers are enticing. Those six months no-interest offers have a way of ruining my budget, so my new mantra is "no thank you."

## Starting Over

You have probably heard it said that you don't begin recovering until you have hit bottom. I sincerely hope this is not necessary for you. If you have gone through complete destruction of your credit and lost your marriage as a result, had your home foreclosed, and see no recovery in sight, you have a long road before you. But if you are still in the middle of the cycle of financial despair, it can be much easier to recover.

In either case, you need to simply start over. Don't dwell on the idea of *failure*, because that is self-destructive. That voice inside your head can be crueler than the worst critic you will meet elsewhere, but it is important to put it all aside and ignore that negative voice. This isn't just hype about feeling good about yourself; it's more about being a grown-up and making a courageous decision today to take a new path in your life and clean up whatever financial mess you may be experiencing.

You need to develop a specific action plan. It includes at least three major points:

1. *Reestablish and rebuild your credit.* This is always the essential first step. No matter what negative items are on your report, the sooner you begin to repair the problem, the sooner the date arrives when those items will be deleted from your report. As part of this, you need to immediately fix the problems that remain. If you have outstanding accounts in arrears, you have to get them caught up. If you have to negotiate with your credit providers to suspend interest, you need to take that step right away.

   Another step is to begin a new credit history from today, which is "day one" in the process. Even if you can no longer qualify for the usual type of credit card, you can get a small-balance secured credit card. These are secured by a fund you keep in a savings account available to the credit card company. If you don't make your payments, they can take those

191

accounts over. These accounts are for anyone who cannot qualify otherwise, but keeping them open for the next year starts establishing a better record. Of course, you *must* make all payments on time. So it helps rebuild your credit to set up a secured credit card and use it regularly. This demonstrates that you are capable of managing credit.

Set up secured bank loans, if you can. These are practically no-risk for the lender. The usual method involves putting a savings account up as security, meaning you cannot use those funds. The account is put aside to protect the bank. Again, you must make all of your payments on time. This can be a one-year loan with monthly payments, which—like secured credit cards—proves that you can plan ahead and make scheduled payments on time. But remember, there can be no excuses. Even one late payment subverts the plan. You must consistently make your payments on time, or you will just be starting over again next year.

If you do not want to use a savings account, you can set up a secured loan and pledge a certificate of deposit(CD), as security. That accomplishes the same outcome, but you will need to make your payments on time just as you do with secured credit cards or bank accounts.

You also rebuild your credit by continuing to make your house payments on time if you are obligated under a mortgage. In addition, you should remain current on all existing credit cards and revolving credit debts. Pay off as much of your debt as you can, and do not be late with any payments. If this requires you to take a second job working nights and weekends, you have to be willing to make that commitment until you are in control. I do not believe in cutting up all of your credit cards and living your life debt-free. That is not realistic. I do believe in establishing and maintaining a realistic and manageable level of credit. Remember, regardless of which of these types of accounts you decide to use to rebuild your credit, it's imperative that you confirm, up front, that the creditor reports to all three credit bureaus. If you obtain a secured card with a creditor that doesn't report, it does nothing to re-establish your credit profile or your credit scores.

2. *Maintain your recovery plan, understanding how long it takes to recover.* You cannot completely recover in only a few months. You need to make a long-term commitment to this process, but it is not a quick fix. If anyone tells you that for a fee they can quickly repair your credit, it is simply not true.

   It takes at least two years after a Chapter 7 bankruptcy before you can see much improvement in your credit score, and this will occur only if you take steps to rebuild without any further mishaps. Also, avoid inquiries and ensure that your balance to credit line ratios remain as low as possible. For Chapter 13 bankruptcy, credit scores should begin to improve as soon as the discharge process is completed. Overall, bankruptcy will remain on your credit report for 10 years.

   After foreclosure, do not expect to see any improvement in your credit score for at least three years from the date the bank sells the foreclosed home. You will need to wait the full three years before applying for a new mortgage.

3. *Look at the situation through a lender's eyes.* If you look at your situation from a lender's point of view, you gain insights into why past due payments after bankruptcy are often treated as the kiss of death. Your fresh start is a second chance in every respect, so if you fail to keep your obligations up to date, why should you be given a third chance?

That's the simple reality. Once you have begun your recovery from poor credit, bankruptcy, or foreclosure, remember that in a very real sense, a second chance is also your last chance. Don't despair if your credit is in terrible shape; once you begin the process it will improve gradually over several years. The most recent 12 months are the most important, which means that as long as you keep everything up to date, the negative items from your past begin to fade in importance and impact. Make sure that you have at the very minimum 12 months of perfect pay history before you apply for any new credit.

Also remember that when you have maxed out a line of credit and are at capacity for a card, that is a big red flag, a sign that you are overextended. This is the guideline you need to follow: Only use your card to the extent that you can afford to pay off the entire balance every month (except for emergencies, of course). Make those payments on time, and value the line of credit as a form of financial freedom. But only use the amount you can afford.

## One Day at a Time—Maintaining Financial Health

To establish increasingly good credit scores, you need to maintain your situation diligently. This is a process you must execute one day at a time. Financial health is like physical health. It requires preventive measures, periodic checkups, and immediate action when problems are discovered.

To maintain your financial health, remember these four guidelines:

1. *Subscribe to a credit-monitoring service and keep it indefinitely.* You must know what is going on with your credit score on a recurring basis. When you are in the process of repairing your credit, you cannot afford to wait a year before ordering a report. You need to be alerted any time something changes on your report. This not only keeps you in touch, but also prevents identity theft or errors.

2. *Never become complacent.* You cannot just repair your credit score and then fall back on old bad habits. You need to take steps to make sure that you learn all about credit, improve your money management habits, and honestly review the way you view credit. In the United States, where there is much financial illiteracy, many people simply don't understand how credit works. This is aggravated by the bad example set by federal and state governments, which seem to always live

beyond their means. If you expect to take control of your financial life and gain the financial freedom you want, you also need to educate yourself.

3. *Remember that you are accountable (but you might need help).* Set specific goals to pay down debts, close accounts, and radically change the way that you use credit. As you learn how to take control, you may need professional help: a qualified attorney, accountant, real estate agent, financial planner, and anyone else who can help will make the process easier. But ultimately *you* are the only one who can change your financial life.

4. *Create a home office and formalize your money management process.* Keep all of your bills and checks in one place, and set regular weekly hours when you are going to review and make payments as required. Appoint a family CFO—which usually stands for chief financial officer but is here extended to also mean credit and finance officer—to manage the process. More than anything else, a married couple needs to make sure they are on the same page and pursuing the same goals. If one of you is diligently paying off credit cards while the other is going to the mall and making purchases, you will never get out of trouble. This is a deal breaker. You both have to agree to communicate honestly and pledge to set financial goals you must reach. The CFO is responsible for taking the right steps (paying bills, reviewing budgets, communicating) to make sure the unified approach is maintained over a long period of time.

## Controlling Your Financial Destiny

The processes you have to go through to repair your credit and to change your methods of operation are absolutely necessary in order for you to control your financial future. If you do not include radical change in your process, it's not going to work.

Remember, this is a form of financial survival, not a debate over who is right or wrong. If a negative item on your credit report for a $50 dispute is affecting your credit, stop trying to be right, and just pay it off. Your credit score is much more important than winning an argument with a merchant, an ex-spouse, or anyone else. This is not about being right; it's about doing the right thing.

You are also going to need to abandon any self-destructive attitudes or arguments. If you think you have been a victim and that is what led to your money problems, you might be right. But you can't benefit from thinking like a victim. The past does not matter, and as long as you think of yourself as a victim, you are not going to be able to take control. Victims, by definition, are helpless. If you feel that way, you should get angry, right now. Stop feeling helpless, and take control of your own destiny. Never again should you wait for bad things to happen to you. From today forward, you have to take firm and decisive steps to ensure that no financial problems occur in the future. *You* are in command, not anyone else.

Just as bad as being a victim is feeling overwhelmed and helpless. Remember that credit scores reflect the present, but they change every day. No problem, no matter how severe, is insurmountable. Some credit problems take longer to repair, but there are no credit issues that cannot be fixed. Anything is possible, and that's the most promising and exciting point I can tell you.

## Stories of Success

Some of the real-life stories I've provided in past chapters were depressing or discouraging. This was necessary to drive home the point about how serious problems are, especially when no steps are taken to prevent or to fix them. But now I want to end with two inspiring true stories about people who recovered from bad experiences, and who changed their lives by taking the right steps.

### Story #1: Trust but First, Verify

In an earlier chapter, I went through the importance of checking a prospective spouse's credit history *before* getting married. That's a good example of how you can avoid failure with a little homework. I got a letter from one of my radio listeners that made this point:

Rodney,

I know that education is your passion, and there are so many people coming to you for help, it's impossible to remember everyone. I wanted to take a minute to thank you for opening my eyes and saving me from making a very big mistake. I had just become engaged to be married, and was excited about making wedding plans and starting our lives together. I think God was looking out for me, though, because I was listening to your radio show one morning, and a light clicked on for me.

I heard you talking about how important it is to know not only your own credit, but also to know the credit of the person you're marrying before tying the knot. I felt like you were talking to *me*, and when the lady gave the date of the credit workshop, I wrote it down, not knowing if I'd really go, but just in case. I dragged my fiancé along, although he didn't really see the point.

During the presentation, you specifically said to pull both credit reports and look at them together before getting married. I wondered why my fiancé was opposed to doing this (he said it didn't matter—we were marrying for love, not credit), but I insisted. Well, I found out *why* he didn't want me to pull it. Although he had told me that he'd never been married and had no children, there was a child support judgment on his credit from the State of Georgia. He denied it at first, and I really wanted to believe him. But when I did some more digging, I found out that not only had he been married before *and* had a seven-year-old child in Georgia, but that he had been arrested for credit card fraud.

My heart was broken, but I broke up with him and moved on—how could I possibly forgive those kind of lies? Thanks to your advice, I found out early and was able to save myself a lot of heartache later. He was not Mr. Right. He was Mr. Wrong, and I wouldn't have known if I hadn't turned your show on that morning.

She was one of the lucky ones who found out what she needed to know *before* moving ahead in blind love. So many others have made the mistake of marrying the wrong person, or having someone destroy their credit, or simply spending more than they could afford. If any of these things have happened to you, don't lose hope. You can recover.

### Story # 2: It Doesn't Help to Avoid the Problem

I heard from a client who could have avoided a lot of grief if she had only paid for a subscription to a credit monitoring service early on. She wrote to me:

Dear Rodney,

My husband and I moved to Dallas from Arizona in 2007. We didn't know the area very well, so decided to rent for awhile so that we could research schools for our daughter and decide on a neighborhood. The house we chose was very nice, but we found out quickly that it wasn't the area for us. There were people out in the street at all hours of the night, and we actually heard gunfire on the weekends—come to find out, there were gangs in the area. I was terrified. I have never been a paranoid person, but couldn't relax in that house. My little girl was only six, and even though the school was only three blocks away, we were afraid to let her walk even that far.

We decided we needed to move, and someone at my husband's office said we should call you. I was really nervous about our credit, but we had to find a better place to live. When I called your office, the lady who pulled our credit report told us that we couldn't be approved because of some late payments and collections that had happened when my daughter was sick, and then when we relocated because my husband didn't have a paycheck for over a month during that time. Instead of just telling us "no," you and your staff listened to our story and began working with us to get our credit in order so that we could get approved to buy a house and get out of this rent house. I know it wasn't easy.

We moved balances around to fix our capacity (we would never have even known what that was). You gave us the tools we needed to negotiate collection accounts and pay them off, but also to get them to remove the paid collections from our credit report! It took nine months of working together to make it happen, but *it worked*. I cried when the new credit was pulled, and we were approved! The home we bought is in a safe, quiet neighborhood. I'm so glad those days of gunfire and fear of going outdoors are over. In a world where people are just a credit score, you took the time to get to know us, gave us the direction and support we needed, and told us that "anything is possible." I truly believe that you saved our family. Thank you!

Imagine how much easier this situation would have been had they only had a credit monitoring system in place to catch these issues before they became big problems. The monthly fee is a small investment to protect a valuable asset—your credit.

## Having Good Credit Improves Your Quality of Life

Having good credit is one of the most important forms of freedom. In a country like the United States, where the concepts of freedom of speech, freedom of religion, and freedom of thought have become buzzwords for anything people want, many of us have lost sight of what freedom really means. If you have poor credit, you have no freedom. You cannot get more credit, qualify for the best mortgage rates, or even buy a home, and you might not even be able to get the job you want. Your credit score is your financial report card in a society based on quantified values and risks.

Think of improving your credit history as a method of bringing up your grade and winning more freedom in your future. After all, without freedom your life is one of restriction and limits. With freedom, anything is possible.

# About the Author

**Rodney Anderson** is a recognized personal finance expert, consumer advocate, and active member of YPO International. His broad knowledge and expertise extends to all aspects of financial well-being, as well as the adversity that many consumers face. He is a regular guest on national and local television and radio, including Fox News, CNBC, MSNBC, and Fox Business News Channel, discussing personal finance, the economy, and industry-related topics.

Rodney is the creator of the Medical Debt Relief Act of 2009, a bill that was recently introduced to Congress by Representative Mary Jo Kilroy (D-OH) and introduced to the Senate by Senator Jeff Merkley (D-OR). This bill was created to protect consumers from suffering long-term effects of medical collection debt. The passing of this bill will mandate that, once a medical collection is paid or settled, it will be completely removed from the consumer's credit report within 30 days.

One of the most prolific mortgage professionals for more than 25 years, Rodney is the country's number one producer of FHA/VA loans, and the second-highest originator of overall mortgage loans in the United States.

Rodney's expertise stems from 25 years' experience and what he calls a "working laboratory of consumer finances." In the past five years alone, Rodney has personally reviewed over 100,000 credit reports and evaluated the personal finances of countless individuals. It is through this information that Rodney has devised strategies and formulas for lasting financial health. Rodney's knowledge

## ABOUT THE AUTHOR

spans economic trends, consumer credit, credit capacity, all types of mortgages, housing markets, and economic indicators, as well as the impact of real-life issues such as spending habits, marriage, divorce, bankruptcy, and foreclosure on individual finances.

Rodney remains active at the grassroots level as an Executive Director with Supreme Lending, located in Plano, Texas, where he assists and counsels thousands of individuals each year. A father of two young adults, Rodney lives with his wife, Kim, in Dallas.

# Index

Acceleration, 150
Action plan for collections, 99–104
  debt payment, 100–101
  debt settlement, 100–101
  repayment plan, 100–101
Addiction to shopping, 21–39
Address change, 89, 103
American Express, 43–44
Assumable loans, 135
Attorneys
  bankruptcy, 156, 185–186
  divorce, 80, 81, 82–83
  selection of, 93
Automated teller machines
    (ATMs), 50–51
  and credit cards, 50–61
  pin numbers, 92
  service and cost comparison,
    53–54

Back taxes, 66
Bad advice, 1–4, 11–13
Bait and switch, 4–6, 134
Balance inquiry fees, 51
Bank accounts, individual, 92
Bankruptcies, 99
  as alternative to foreclosures,
    156–157

early action advantage, 187–188
horror stories about, 184
medical debt as cause of, 110
need for, 178–182
origins of, 176–178
process of, 186–187
self assessment regarding, 179–180
steps to take, 183–186
types of, 182–183
Bankruptcy attorney, 156
  selection of, 185–186
Banks, unfair practices, 48–49
Bidding, 33
Bill organization, 71
Bill payments, 70–72
Budget busters, 142–144
Budget setting, 72–73
Buyer beware, 145

Cash advances, 54
Cash payments, 54
Chapter 7 bankruptcy, 182, 193
Chapter 11 bankruptcy, 183
Chapter 13 bankruptcy, 157,
    182–183, 193
Checking accounts
  individual vs. joint, 69–70
  separate, 59

Child support, 75, 76
Closing costs, 132
Closing dates, 134
Collection agencies, 99
Collection calls, 108–109
Collections, 95–111
   action plan for, 99–104
   credit card agencies, 104–109
   debt settlement agencies,
      104–109
   medical emergencies, 109–111
   origins of, 177
   records correction, 96–98
   seven-year rule, 98–99
   steps to take, 103–104
Commute costs, 144
Consumer debt, 42
Convenience of shopping, 30–31
Cookies (browser), 27–30, 35–36
Cosigned debts, 68
Credit capacity, 45, 54–55, 117,
   120, 180
Credit Card Accountability,
   Responsibility, and Disclosure
   Act of 2009, 48
Credit card agencies, 104–109
Credit card statements, 67
Credit cards, 17, 41–56
   American Express, 43–44
   and ATMs, 50–61
   double billing, 170
   education on, 51–54
   laws regarding, 48
   minimum monthly payment,
      46–47
   pin numbers, 92
   as plastic dynamite, 43

   providers of, 43–45
   risks from, 43
   rules for, 190
   rules regarding, 45–46
   unfair practices, 48–49
Credit chasing, 17, 45
Credit data, 119
Credit history length, 121
Credit inquiries, 121, 124, 125
Credit limit, 180
Credit monitoring system, 91, 126,
   198, 199
Credit obligations, 90
Credit rejection, 85
Credit repair, 105
Credit repair agencies, 107
Credit report agencies, 107–108
Credit reports, 118–121, 191–194
   error rate, 113
   fraud alert on, 93
   impact of shopping, 26–27
   joint review of, 65
   pulling and reviewing, 125
Credit score, 45
   after Chapter 7 bankruptcy, 193
   after Chapter 13 bankruptcy,
      193
   meaning of, 115–118
   and overspending, 39
Credit score methods, 118–121
Credit scoring
   affecting insurance rates, 163
   affecting interest rate, 137
Credit scoring criteria, 120–121
Credit scoring system, myths
   regarding, 115–118
Credit system

credit score, meaning of,
115–118
credit score methods, 118–121
horror stories about, 123–125
strategies for control, 125–127
your credit report, 118–121
Credit types, 121
Credit-monitoring service, 194
Customer service, 34

Damage control
identity theft, 168–169
identity theft, vulnerability to,
169–173
insurance policies, agents review,
162–164
insurance policies, components
of, 160–162
insurance policies, cost of,
159–160
investments, 164–167
Dating interview tips, 60–64
Debit cards, 14, 49, 54
Debt level, 182
Debt repayment, 125
Debt responsibility, 85
Debt settlement, 100–101
Debt settlement agencies, 104–109
Department store credit cards,
50, 53
Direct deposits, 92
Disclosures, 61
Divorce, 18, 181
fifteen steps going through,
89–93
financial separation, 82–83
and mortgage obligations, 76

spousal behavior during, 80–82
Divorce attorneys
financial counseling, 80, 81
selection of, 82–83
Divorce decrees, 75
Divorce petition, 91
Do not call letter, 108
Dormant account fee, 55

eBay, 25
Education on credit cards, 51–54
Equifax address, 106
Eviction, 150
Experian address, 106

Fair Credit Reporting Act, 99, 116
Fair Debt Collection Practices Act,
99, 108–109
FAKO (credit scoring system), 120
Family CFO, 72
Family CFO (chief financial
officer), 20, 70, 72, 159, 195
Family CIO (chief investment
officer), 165
Family law practitioners, 83
Federal lien, 150
Federal Reserve Board Regulation
B, 119
Fee structure of financial
advisors, 12
FICO (credit scoring system),
115, 120
Financial action plan, 191–194
Financial advisors, 3–4, 6
bankruptcies help, 184
fee structure, 12
selection of, 166–167

Financial alienation syndrome, 87
Financial divorce, 93
Financial life, 189–200
  credit monitoring program,
    198–199
  financial destiny, 195–196
  financial health, 194–195
  financial illiteracy, 194
  financial literacy, 189–190
  good credit and quality of life,
    199–200
  starting over, 191–194
  success stories, 196–200
  trust but verify approach,
    196–198
Fine print, 34–35, 52
Float-down option, 136
Foreclosures, 140
  avoidance of, 151–157
  bankruptcy as alternative to,
    156–157
  basics, 149–151
  impact of, 157–158
  by judicial sale, 149
  loan modification, 153–154
  short sales, 155–156
401(k) plans/accounts, 152–153,
    155–156
Fraud alert on credit report, 93
Full disclosure, 57
  marriage, 57–59

Good credit and quality of life,
  199–200
Good faith estimate, 133, 134
Good Faith Estimate Truth in
  Lending disclosure, 134

Google search results, 28
Grace periods, 52
Gutierrez, Luis, 110

Hard pulls, 125
Health insurance and benefits,
  73–74
Home inspection, 141–142
Home rental, 154
Home sale, 154
Homeowner's insurance, 15, 160
Home Owners Association
  (HOA), 144
Homestead exemption for real
  estates, 157
Horror stories
  about action plan for collections,
    102–103
  about bankruptcies, 184
  about convenient subscription
    deal, 123
  about credit cards, 47–48
  about credit system, 123–125
  about inquiry effect, 123–125
Hours of shopping, 23–26

Identity theft, 87, 93, 168–169,
  194
  reporting, 172–173
  vulnerability to, 169–173
Impulse purchases, 16, 21, 30
Income stability, 77
Inquiry effect, 123–125
Insurance agents, 15
Insurance coverage, 161–162, 163
Insurance policies
  agents review, 162–164

components of, 160–162
cost, of, 159–160
Interest rates, 133
  credit scoring affecting, 137
  lock agreement, 136
Introductory rates, 41, 52
Investments, 164–167
IRS liens, 150

Job history, 77
Job loss, 181
Joint accounts, 87, 91
Joint bank accounts, 92
Joint checking account, 66
Joint credit report, 90
Joint debts, 82
Judgments, 67, 99
Judicial sale, 149

Kilroy, Mary Jo, 110

Late fees, 67, 180
Laws regarding credit cards, 48
Lawyers. *See* attorneys
Lender questions, 133–137
Lenders, contact with, 152
Liens, 149
Loan modification, 153–154
Loan refinancing, 135
Loans for real estate, 132–137

Mall cops, 37–38
Marketing, reality of, 23
Marriage, 57–78
  dating interview tips, 60–64
  full disclosure, 57–59
  ten steps before, 64–78

Medical bills, 74, 181
Medical debt as cause of
  bankruptcies, 110
Medical Debt Relief Act of
  2009, 108
Medical emergencies, 109–111
Minimum monthly payment,
  46–47, 53
Money management, 195
Monthly cash flow, 53
Myths regarding credit scoring
  system, 115–118

Need vs. want, 30

Online auction bidding, 33–34
Online availability limitation,
  36–37
Online gambling, 26
Online shopping, ease of, 24–26
Open houses, 138
Options adjustable-rate mortgage
  (ARM), 130
Overdraft fees, 14, 49
Overspending and credit score, 39
Owner-occupied vs. ownership, 140

Pay as you go concept, 33
Payment history, 120
Payments for shopping, 32
Post office box, 103
Predatory advice, 12
Predatory calls, 28
Premiums, 160
Prepaid gift cards, 51
Prepayment penalty, 135
Prepayment penalty clause, 131

Price comparison, 38–39
Private mortgage insurance, 151
Professional subprime advice, 11
Property taxes, 131, 143
Public records, 65–66

Real estate, 129–145
  about, 129–132
  budget busters, 142–144
  buyer beware, 145
  homestead exemption for, 157
  loans for, 132–137
  real estate agents, 137–142
Real estate agents, 137–142
  experience, 139
  litmus test for, 138–141
  local knowledge, 141
  part-time, 139
Real Estate Settlement Procedures
  Act (RESPA), 134
Records correction, 96–98
Recourse debt, 151
Refinancing, 26–27, 87
Regulation B, 119
Repayment plan, 100–101
Responsibility, 8–9
Reward points and miles, 44
Risks from credit cards, 43
Rules regarding credit cards,
  45–46

Secured loans, 192
Seduction of shopping, 21–23
Sensitive information, 172
Seven-year rule, 98–99
Shopping
  addiction, 21–39

convenience of, 30–31
cookies (browser), 27–30,
  35–36
credit report impact of, 26–27
fine print, 34–35
hours of, 23–26
impulse purchases, 30
mall cops, 37–38
need vs. want, 30
online auction bidding,
  33–34
online availability limitation,
  36–37
payments for, 32
price comparison, 38–39
seduction, 21–23
vulnerable situation for, 32
Shopping hours, 24
Shopping list, 38
Short sales, 155–156
Site blocking, 36–37
Spending
  out-of-control, 39
  vs. saving, 23
Starting over, 191–194
Statistics, 10–11
Strategies for control of credit
  system, 125–127
Subprime advice, 11–12
Success stories, 196–200

Tax liens, 66, 99
Taxation of short sales, 156
Taxes on write-offs, 99
Teaser loan rates, 52
Temporary restraining order
  (TRO), 91

# Index

Ten steps before marriage, 64–78
Terms and conditions, 52
Title search, 150
Trans Union address, 106
Trigger leads, 28
Trust but verify approach, 58,
      196–198

Unfair practices with credit cards,
      48–49
Utility bills, 141, 142, 143

Verification steps, 97

Window-shopping, 38